Words of Management Wisdom

Book 1 – Starting Out

Words of Management Wisdom

Book 1 – Starting Out

WILLIAM P. FISHER, PH.D.

THOMSON
━━━━━✦━━━━━ ™
DELMAR LEARNING

Australia Canada Mexico Singapore Spain United Kingdom United States

THOMSON

DELMAR LEARNING

Winning Wizard's Words of Management Wisdom
Book 1: Starting Out

William P. Fisher, Ph.D.

Vice President, Career Education SBU:
Dawn Gerrain

Director of Learning Solutions:
Sherry Gomoll

Managing Editor:
Robert L. Serenka, Jr.

Acquisitions Editor:
Martine Edwards

Editorial Assistant:
Jennifer Anderson

Director of Production:
Wendy A. Troeger

Production Manager:
J.P. Henkel

Production Editor:
Rebecca Goldthwaite

Director of Marketing:
Wendy E. Mapstone

Channel Manager:
Gerard McAvey

Marketing Coordinator:
Erica Conley

Cover & Text Design:
essence of 7

Library of Congress Cataloging-in-Publication Data

Fisher, William P.
   Winning wizard's words of management wisdom: starting out / by William P. Fisher.-- 1st ed.
      p. cm.
   Includes index.
   ISBN-13: 978-1-4018-1560-8 (alk. paper)
   1. Leadership. 2. Executive ability. 3. Creative ability in business. 4. Organizational effectiveness. I. Title.
   HD57.7.F5834 2005
   658.4'092--dc22

                  2005028444

Contents

About the Author

William P. Fisher, Ph.D., is the Darden Eminent Scholar Chair in restaurant management in the Rosen College of Hospitality Management at the University of Central Florida in Orlando. He previously held positions as the chief executive officer of the American Hotel & Lodging Association and the National Restaurant Association, both based in Washington, D.C. He also was the executive vice president of finance and administration for a major food service contract management organization.

He holds three degrees from Cornell University: a B.S. in hotel administration, an M.B.A. (finance), and a Ph.D. in educational administration.

His academic credentials include service as an assistant professor in the school of hotel administration, where he taught accounting, finance, and management courses. He was a partner in the consulting firm of Gaurnier Associates simultaneously with his teaching responsibilities.

The author of numerous articles and books, Dr. Fisher was recognized as "Champion of Education" by the Council on Hotel, Restaurant, and Institutional Education (CHRIE) in 1996 and is the first recipient of the Michael E. Hurst Lifetime Achievement in Education Award, bestowed by the Education Foundation of the National Restaurant Association.

Married for more than 40 years, he and his wife, Yvonne, have three children and nine grandchildren.

Embarkation

L ONG AGO AND FAR AWAY, in the land of Yenom, there lived an eager young management trainee by the name of Redael. Anxious to embark on a fulfilling career, Redael thought it prudent to seek advice and counsel from organizational elders as to what was necessary to ensure career success. Moving from one departmental chieftain to another in search of guidance and insights, Redael was rebuffed time and time again as the chieftains claimed "busy schedule" as the reason to decline appointments.

In the most recent attempt, the Human Resources chieftain mentioned that Redael should really talk with the organization's Winning Wizard (now retired) who was in his office in the Stratospheric Suite on the top floor.

Excited by this possibility, Redael visited the office of Winning Wizard, explaining the nature of the request.

"Well, Redael," drawled Winning Wizard, "I will meet with you because you are new to the organization, but only if you are sincere in taking to mind and heart what I will tell you. Agreed?"

"Absolutely!" exclaimed Redael. "I will devote my full attention to the words of wisdom you dispense."

"Good," confirmed Winning Wizard. "Then we shall begin.

"As you are just starting out, realize that you have many working years ahead of you. Whatever you do, wherever you go, for however long, you need to fully commit to your assignment and to your organization. You can't be tentative, lackadaisical, or easily distracted. You need to keep focus, remain intense, and develop a 'success' demeanor.

"I'll sum up your first lesson with

THE WIZARD'S WORDS OF MANAGEMENT WISDOM #1

Put your heart in your organization and your organization in your heart. Put your mind on your assignment, and keep your assignment on your mind."

"Good thoughts, Winning Wizard," Redael said. "This is exciting."

Climbing
an Organizational
Mountain

"AS YOU START OUT IN your career, Redael," waxed Winning Wizard, settling comfortably into a mentorship role, "you should realize that there is a striking parallel between climbing an organizational mountain and climbing a terrestrial mountain. Allow me to explain.

"If you intend to reach the summit, you must plan carefully, prepare well, secure the best equipment possible, know how and when to use that equipment, and surround yourself with other expert climbers. You must train both physically and mentally and seek advice from others who have made the climb before you. You'll need to maintain that single-mindedness of purpose—that the apex is the ultimate goal. History rarely recognizes organizational mountain climbers who are satisfied with scaling only half a mountain."

"Go on Winning Wizard," Redael said excitedly. "I find this fascinating!"

Winning Wizard smiled as he continued, "When starting out, you cannot be profligate with your resources or you'll not have them when you need them. You cannot be reckless or careless at lower levels or you will be doomed almost before you start. Besides, Redael, you don't want that kind of reputation.

"You need to follow your basic plan. Once initiated, your climb should be doggedly progressive, not wavering from loss of spirit or stamina. As you ascend the organizational mountain the air becomes thinner and you will not cover the distance at higher levels that you did earlier within comparable timeframes. Higher elevations give you a better view, but they require greater surety of movement. You've got to be in shape! The atmosphere gets colder, the ground can become slippery, and storms do occur. You will need some insulation, but it can't be so tight that it cuts off circulation. Thick skin helps!"

"I'm taking copious notes, Winning Wizard," said Redael, writing hurriedly, "Go ahead."

Winning Wizard continued, "At the higher levels, each additional step has to be considered carefully before it is taken. The safety line to the fall-back position must be absolutely secure. Risks will be encountered, and the unexpected will happen. Don't be immobilized by it. You can overcome unsettling occurrences using your resourcefulness and creativity. You must realize that you and others in your climbing party are interdependent.

"As you continue your ascent, the details of lower altitudes lose focus out of sheer distance. You must expect that and cannot lament it. You should not step upward while looking downward or your balance will be in jeopardy. Still, you must be mindful of the conditions below you.

"At the highest elevations, the view is exhilarating and the sense of accomplishment is momentous. Never forget, however, that it takes one set of talents to get to the top, but some additional talents and resources are needed to remain there for any period of time. You may also feel a bit isolated from time to time, but that's the price you pay for your abilities. At some point, you will leave the summit. It's just a question of whether you will step aside, step down, or fall down."

"That's fantastic, Winning Wizard," marveled Redael, "I have a clear understanding now of what it takes and what I need to do. I can't wait to get started."

"That's a good attitude to have, Redael," Winning Wizard said, "but there's a lot more you need to know. Allow me to summarize this point with

THE WIZARD'S WORDS OF MANAGEMENT WISDOM #2

If you are going to climb an organizational mountain, you've got to know the ropes!"

Management ABCs

"**M**ANAGEMENT, REDAEL, IS AT once simple and complex. It is simple in concept and complex in conduct. Let's talk about the easy side first," extolled Winning Wizard. "I refer to these virtues as the management ABCs. There is such a thing as alphabet management, which is what you want to develop. Then again, there is malphabet management, which, unfortunately, a lot of unsuccessful managers have developed. Here are both the virtues and the vices."

ALPHABET MANAGEMENT

Attitude—It all starts here. Get a good one and never let it go!

Brightness—This covers both mental ability and personality. Sparkle!

Competence—It's the name of the game. Go for it!

Decisiveness—Leaders act and don't look back!

Effectiveness—Making an impact means making a difference!

Flexibility—If you can't bend, you'll snap!

Glibness—One who speaks well sells well. You're always selling!

Honesty—By definition, any deviance from total honesty is some degree of dishonesty!

Innovation—Create creativity creatively!

Judgment—Call 'em like you see 'em, but be sure you see 'em!

Knowledge—Know the organization, know the industry, know yourself!

Loyalty—It runs down as well as up!

Methodical—Remember the tortoise and the hare?

Noble—If it's the right thing to do, do it right!

Objectivity—Think with your mind, not your heart!

Productivity—Produce productivity productively!

Quality mindedness—This gives definition to your existence!

Resilience—No matter how hard the hit, you can come back!

Sensitivity—You're part of the world, not the center of it!

Tenacity—The best decisions come from determined dedication!

Understanding—Mistakes will be made but should not be repeated!

Vision—It goes beyond 'mission'; it's organizational self-actualization!

Wisdom—This is intelligence supported by experience, ethics, and a moral core!

Xenophilia—Openness to others is the essence of graciousness!

Yeastiness—The best way to rise is to keep the organization rising!

Zeal—Be twice as good as yesterday and half as good as tomorrow!

MALPHABET MANAGEMENT

"These are some of the vices you want to avoid, Redael," Winning Wizard admonished, "They are career killers."

Arrogance—Life is to serve others, not humble them!

Belligerence—If you're going to fight, be prepared to lose!

Crudity—Being crude is the pits, and that's where it belongs!

Deception—If you lose your trustworthiness, nothing's left!

Egocentricity—You can't fool those who work for you!

Fatuousness—No one suffers fools very long!

Garrulousness—This person talks a lot and says nothing!

Hostility—If people grate you, you'll never be great!

Inefficiency—Waste hastens you out!

Jealousy—Too bad self-improvement is subordinate to covetousness!

Klutziness—Insensitivity breeds contempt!

Laziness—Remember the hare and the tortoise?

Malevolence—One who is destructive cultivates destructiveness!

Negligence—If you overlook standards, you'll be overrun!

Oppressiveness—Do you really think you're here to hold others back?

Pettiness—This is an anchor on progress!

Quarrelsome—Arguments usually shed more heat than light!

Resentfulness—Life can be unfair, but everyone gets a share of unfairness!

Spitefulness—An eye for an eye makes you both half blind!

Temperamental—Others will brood if you have changing moods!

Uncertainty—Indecision reflects insecurity!

Vindictiveness—Revenge is not becoming; it's debasing!

Wailing—Crying doesn't solve the problem!

Xenophobia—If you don't like people, there's always Mt. Everest!

Yahoo—We can all stand a little more polish and sophistication!

Zaniness—There is a difference in being 'off the plan' and 'off the wall!'

"Summing up, my young colleague, here is

THE WIZARD'S WORDS OF MANAGEMENT WISDOM #3

Know your management ABCs!"

"Right on, Winning Wizard," said a determined Redael. "I'll know the alphabet, and I'll not practice the malphabet."

Real-World Education

"**I** HAVE FOUND, REDAEL," voiced Winning Wizard, "that next to the disciplines of finance and marketing, which are nine-tenths mechanics and one-tenth judgment, the most misunderstood discipline in organizational life is employee development. There are a lot of buzz words in that realm that give rise to confusion and inarticulation. There are 'training programs,' 'internships,' 'development programs,' 'educational programs,' 'empowerment programs,' and scores of other pious-sounding words and phrases, but you need to get behind the words to understand the concept.

"Let me give you

THE WIZARD'S WORDS OF MANAGEMENT WISDOM #4

Education is learning to think, and training is learning to execute."

"That's an interesting distinction, Winning Wizard," said Redael, "but you'd better explain it fully to be sure I've got it."

"I'll give you an illustration, Redael, that I think will clarify the point," said Winning Wizard.

"You can train a dog, for example, to bark, shake hands, roll over, jump up, lie down, and perform any number of tricks. The dog *does* something by *executing* on command. No one, however, would say the dog is 'educated.' They may say the dog is smart, but we don't educate animals, we train them. Conversely, you have and will continue to receive an education, because education is a lifelong process. Education is the process of intellectual development brought about by the infusion of knowledge, analytical skills, creativity skills, and problem-solving techniques. It's the internalization of knowledge, experience, and observation for use at an appropriate time. Education is more than training, because training does not necessarily require thought—reflexes, yes, but not thought!

"My point, my dear Redael, is that you need to be both a thinker and a doer, and moreover, you need to surround yourself with subordinates who are thinking doers. You can't be just one or the other and expect to be upwardly mobile and successful in your career."

"That's good advice, Winning Wizard, and I'll remember that," said Redael, "Is there anything else I need to know about education and training before we move on?"

"Certainly there is, my friend," said Winning Wizard, "You need to understand two more points. The first is

THE WIZARD'S WORDS OF MANAGEMENT WISDOM #5

There is a difference between intelligence and education. A lot of intelligent people don't have an education, and vice versa. Measure yourself and others on intellectual merit, not on educational credentials."

"You're right, Winning Wizard. I've already run into that with some people I know. I'm not the haughty type," pronounced Redael.

"Well, that's good. Just remain that way, even in the presence of pretentious and supercilious people," cautioned Winning Wizard.

"Now let me make my final point with respect to education," said Winning Wizard. "It's expressed best as

THE WIZARD'S WORDS OF MANAGEMENT WISDOM #6

Graduation ceremonies at schools are called 'commencements.' They are not called 'conclusions.'

"Your real-world education is under way because you'll have to apply what you learned in school, and you'll also want to make every day a new learning experience. Education is a process, not a product," concluded Winning Wizard.

"This is great stuff, Winning Wizard. I'm really learning a lot," said an enthused Redael.

Essentially Yours

"**N**OW, REDAEL, LET ME ASK YOU a fundamental question, the answer to which will evoke your basic management philosophy and behavior as perceived by your subordinates," said Winning Wizard with a wry smile.

"Which position is the most important of these three: the manager, the manager's secretary, or the mailroom attendant?"

Suspecting an intellectual trap, Redael paused for a moment and responded in a firm voice, "They are all equally important, Winning Wizard," with an eyebrow slightly raised, expecting approval.

"Oh, really?" scoffed Winning Wizard. "What are you, some sort of an idealist, or did you just finish some sort of Human Relations seminar? If you don't have a sense of reality, you better reconsider your career options."

Now feeling completely ensnared in an intellectual trap, Redael began to backtrack. "Of course, one could argue that the manager is the most important because that position carries the greatest amount of responsibility. After all, organizations are hierarchical structures."

"What?" bellowed Winning Wizard, "You're going to tell the people in the mailroom that their positions are not as important as the secretary or the manager? Suppose everything stopped in the mailroom? How effective would the secretary and the manager be then? Or suppose the secretary stopped completing duties? Do you have any sense of what happens when you have these types of breakdowns?"

Redael, now flushing and perspiring, wilted in confusion. Sensing Redael's frustration, Winning Wizard smiled bemusingly. "Redael, you have just experienced

THE WIZARD'S WORDS OF MANAGEMENT WISDOM #7

Don't answer impossible questions.

"Instead, articulate the real management concept that is being called forth in this example. Let me explain.

"There is no question that there are different levels of responsibility, authority, reward systems, sanctions, and restrictions in any organization, in terms of the requirements and scope of different positions. A manager's position is at a higher level than a secretary, and so on. On the other hand, each job incumbent must perform as prescribed, or the entire organization suffers. Each position, therefore, is essential and interdependent on another as a result of its integration in the overall system. If a position is not essential, abolish it. You're wasting resources if you don't!"

"I guess I really fell into that trap, didn't I?" moaned Redael, feeling a little relieved and returning to normal facial color.

"We're going to sharpen your thinking, Redael, and you will be all the better off for it," said Winning Wizard, locking into eye contact with the young trainee.

"Let me sum up with

THE WIZARD'S WORDS OF MANAGEMENT WISDOM #8

Communicate the essential nature of their positions to your subordinates, both in terms of the requirement for peak performance and in terms of their role in the overall organizational structure.

"Not only do you need to tell them, my dear Redael, but you need to show them by way of your own relationships with them and in terms of your own conduct," Winning Wizard continued. "You need to make them feel they are essential."

"Right!" Redael said with determination. "I'll do that."

Consistently Yours

"**I** WANT TO TELL YOU about a former colleague of mine, Redael," mused Winning Wizard, "to illustrate a point that you should always remember." Winning Wizard pointed to a picture on the credenza of a distinguished-looking executive holding a plaque, the initials on which were readily discernible: "MVP."

"We'll call this executive 'Elbaulav,'" said Winning Wizard, his voice cracking ever so slightly.

"I'm sure the two of you were very close," inserted Redael, feeling the need to acknowledge the apparent emotion of the moment.

Winning Wizard continued, "When Elbaulav first joined the organization, there was no training program. Consequently, no one was well trained. People sort of did their own thing, and work was haphazard at best and counterproductive at worst. Since Elbaulav had no training, his performance was not good, but since the organization still had to function, errors were either overlooked or were remedied by others before they became too serious.

"Employees came and went, but Elbaulav stayed and was eventually promoted to department head on the basis of tenure. Elbaulav always made wrong decisions on business matters, but times were good and the organization seemed to succeed in spite of itself. Moreover, when staff meetings occurred, Elbaulav always seemed to be advocating approaches or courses of action that the organization wound up not pursuing."

Redael was beginning to wonder where this story was going at this point but remained respectfully attentive.

"When I was made Chief Executive Officer, I immediately promoted Elbaulav to be my personal assistant," said Winning Wizard, nodding in self-approval, "You see, Redael, when I was faced with a crucial decision, I would always turn to Elbaulav for advice and counsel. I would then do the *exact opposite* of what Elbaulav recommended, and we became enormously successful. Elbaulav became the most valuable person ever employed by the organization because I could count on Elbaulav *always being wrong*. My point to you, my young friend, can be summed up in

THE WIZARD'S WORDS OF MANAGEMENT WISDOM #9

Consistency can often be as valuable as accuracy."

"That's quite a story with a great moral," Redael said, evidencing awareness of an insight just received.

"Yes it is," said Winning Wizard. "Just think about it for a moment. Accountants are guided by consistency. Advertising needs to be consistent to be effective. The application of human resources policies needs to be consistent, as does the execution of training programs, which, by the way, Elbaulav advised against developing. We went ahead and developed them anyway, as I then knew it was the right thing to do," said Winning Wizard.

"What strikes me about that story, Winning Wizard," ventured Redael, "is that it somehow cheapens the value of accuracy."

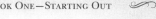

"Good point, Redael. I can tell we are making progress!" exclaimed Winning Wizard. "So let me quickly add

THE WIZARD'S WORDS OF MANAGEMENT WISDOM #10

Accuracy is paramount, but you also need to look
for consistency!

"And, Redael, while we're at it, let me say a word to you about 'policy,'" Winning Wizard stated, visibly enjoying the mentorship role. "It's

THE WIZARD'S WORDS OF MANAGEMENT WISDOM #11

A policy is not a regulation. Policies are guideposts, not
edicts. Apply them as appropriate, but make exceptions when
it's the right thing for the organization to do."

"That's a good distinction, Winning Wizard," Redael noted, "a very good distinction."

Obsession Versus Compulsion

WINNING WIZARD CONTINUED to peer into the eyes of Redael, attempting to discern the seriousness and maturity of the fledgling trainee.

"Tell me, Redael, what is your immediate reaction when I say to you the word 'work?' Is it positive, in that it excites you—do you feel properly challenged and stimulated? Or is it a negative reaction, in that you mentally wince when you hear it and shy away from it or consider it drudgery? I don't expect you to reveal your innermost thoughts to me, but I raise the question to make a point."

"I think I see the point already, Winning Wizard," said Redael, warming to the relationship and the conversation. "If I adopt, as part of my personal and professional philosophy, an attitude that work is there for me to do, that I can make it fun and can cause progress, it's better than considering work a necessary burden and an interruption to the rest of my life," Redael exclaimed, feeling that they were forming a philosophy.

"That's half of it, Redael," said Winning Wizard. "Attitude is the core foundation of every aspect of life, so it's important that you plant and cultivate a good one because that will serve you well in whatever you do. I sum it up with these

THE WIZARD'S WORDS OF MANAGEMENT WISDOM #12

Work is what you get to do, not what you have to do. Go after it and get it. Don't let it elude you. "

"I've got that, Winning Wizard, but if that's only half the point, what's the other half?" queried Redael.

"The other half deals with the people you will be working with because everyone doesn't have a positive attitude and a productive philosophy," said Winning Wizard. "It's a sad fact of life, but, nonetheless, it is still a fact. Because you hope to manage people, you need to recognize this to get maximum performance from them. That's an essential covenant of skillful management."

"Well, what's the answer to managing this, Winning Wizard?" asked Redael, looking perplexed.

"There are a lot of answers, Redael, and we'll get to them, but for now, take to heart

THE WIZARD'S WORDS OF MANAGEMENT WISDOM #13

People work, irrespective of whether their motivation is survival and other economic needs (compulsion) or whether internalized philosophy and lifestyle are the dominant reasons (obsession). The distinction between obsession and compulsion is not always obvious. Irrespective, draw the most, and the best, from each of your employees.

"It's up to you, Redael, to set the conditions that cause people to want to work for you. Allow them to work out of inspiration, not perspiration.

"Let me conclude this part of our discussion with a two-part truism that serves as

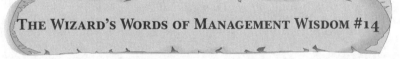

THE WIZARD'S WORDS OF MANAGEMENT WISDOM #14

1. Nothing succeeds like managerial success.

2. The reciprocal is also true: Nothing fails like management failure."

"I'm not afraid of hard work," Redael stated. "If that's what it takes to succeed, then I'm up to it."

Authority!
Responsibility!

"IT'S TIME NOW, REDAEL, to focus on two fundamental management concepts, **authority** and **responsibility**, and the relationship that exists between them.

"The word **authority** has numerous meanings, among which can be listed the following:

1. An expert in one's field
2. Truthfulness, as in 'I have it on good authority'
3. A body or group to which an appeal may be made, such as a review board
4. A person or group who issues and/or enforces rules or laws, such as the legal and justice systems

"I will define authority, Redael, in the organizational sense, as **the vested legal right of a person to use organizational resources to attain organizational objectives.** Resources may consist of time, money, office space, equipment, subordinates, and so forth. Objectives may be to increase sales, increase return on investment, decrease labor turnover, increase productivity, and on and on.

"**Responsibility** is another word with several meanings, among which can be included the following:

1. Capability of responding
2. Liability, in the judicial and/or financial sense
3. Maturity and conscientiousness, which applies to both people and organizations
4. Accountability, in the financial sense
5. Adherence to the highest of desired values

"Defined in the organizational sense, **responsibility is the relationship existing between the person performing an assignment and the person who imposed that assignment.** If you will accept, Redael, a definition of **management** as 'getting things done with and through others,' then you must accept the principle that a manager must delegate to subordinates in order for the objectives to be reached. Well, that's all well and good, but what is it that the manager delegates—**authority** or **responsibility**?

"Certainly, if you expect someone else to carry out an assignment, that person must have access to the tools and resources necessary to function. The delegatee will use them. You will not because you have granted your subordinate this vested right. Accordingly, we might say that authority, as we have defined it, is what's delegated. But, isn't there also some requirement on the part of the person assigned the task to act responsibly? Logic tells us, 'yes, of course,' so perhaps we should conclude that the subordinate is delegated both authority and responsibility. But not so fast! We've all heard that it is the head of an organization who is ultimately responsible for the organization's performance, and if this is true, the top manager can't delegate this responsibility. Perhaps, then, a subordinate is delegated only authority and not responsibility. Somehow that doesn't seem right either, does it? What about the other alternative? Could a subordinate be delegated the responsibility but not the authority to achieve the goal? No, Redael, that's ridiculous. That situation creates a fiasco.

"Well, Redael, let's take these seemingly complex concepts and boil them down to their core meanings," concluded Winning Wizard. "I'll do that by issuing

THE WIZARD'S WORDS OF MANAGEMENT WISDOM #15

An act of delegation conveys and creates both authority and responsibility with respect to the subordinate. This conveyance/creation continues to each successive level of delegation. As a result, authority may descend in the organization to its point of need, effectiveness, and implementation. Responsibility, however, is accumulated, compounded, and fortified at each level in order of organizational ascension, so that final and ultimate responsibility culminates at the highest organizational level. As authority descends, responsibility ascends."

"That's heavy-duty stuff, Winning Wizard," noted Redael, head shaking in wonderment. "But you're right! You can't delegate responsibility away from you if you are the one in charge."

"You're learning, Redael," smiled Winning Wizard. "You're learning."

Understanding
Authority

"**A**UTHORITY IS A MUCH USED and much abused word, Redael," sighed Winning Wizard, "and not many people understand it as a basis for power and a force for actions. You need to fully understand it, my friend, in order to use it properly."

"OK," said Redael. "I hadn't given it much thought before, so I really should bear down on it, shouldn't I?"

"Yes," said Winning Wizard, "and I'll start by telling you there are six types of authority; none of them necessarily mutually exclusive. That is to say, they can all exist in combination with one another. I'll take you through them.

1. **Coercion authority** is the use of physical force or the threat thereof to compel obedience and/or repress activity. At the height of a disagreement, you may have heard a superior say to a subordinate, or vice versa, 'Let's go outside and settle this once and for all,' as though pure physical dominance would transfer to the organizational relationship. It also happens that an organizational superior can exert a Svengalian mind control over a subordinate to the degree that the subordinate is a mental

slave to the master superordinate. The forcing of one's will on another to do something illegal or contrary to company policy, for example, is a case of mental coercion. This is the rawest form of authority and should rarely, if ever, be used in an organizational context.

2. **Resource authority** involves the allocation and interplay of organizational resources from a superordinate to a subordinate. Budget allocations, information flow, office space assignments, bonuses, promotions, and numerous other examples of resources can be meted out, or withheld, by using resource authority. I've always found it somewhat amusing how nice some people are to others in the organization, irrespective of title or position, if they believe there is a current or potential resource allocation benefit that could involve them," said Winning Wizard, somewhat sardonically.

3. **Legal authority** is the most rational and common base found in organizations. It provides a vested right by law, organizational by-law, charter, or policy to engage in an activity. Most organizations and professions need a certificate or license from a governmental agency that empowers them to operate. At the individual level the appointment or promotion of a person is the organizational legality that gives the designee the right to function and use resources pertinent to the position. Press releases announcing promotions or appointments are more than motivational and recognition courtesies. They alert the world that the designee is now the person with whom to relate if one's needs encompass the designee's office.

4. **Identification authority** is the charisma or magnetism of the individual that gives that individual influence over others. When someone has 'it,' others admire it and are inspired by it, which causes subordinates, or a constituency, to do what the charismatic individual wants done. Politicians, as one example, often rely heavily on identification authority for their base of power.

5. **Expertise authority** is simply the combination of knowledge and experience applied to a given situation. If you know what you are doing and others don't, then you possess expertise authority over them because you are the possessor of the relevant knowledge and experience. When a vehicle breaks down, for example, the mechanic who can fix it has the expertise authority, irrespective of the lofty positions or titles of the passengers.

6. **Cultural authority** varies, depending on the culture and the environment. It's an authority born of deference to a group or individual, based on the customs and mores of that society. Some societies venerate the elderly, some venerate females, while others venerate males or the oldest male or female heir. Authority attaches to members of the group the culture deems worthy of authority influence.

"Well, Redael, where does all this lead us, with respect to the lessons we can draw from this discussion?" inquired Winning Wizard.

"That's quite an analysis," said Redael. "How do you best sum it up?"

"Let me do it with

THE WIZARD'S WORDS OF MANAGEMENT WISDOM #16

"Of the six types of authority, coercion is the most repugnant, resource authority is the most susceptible to manipulation, legal authority is the strongest and most civilized, identification authority is the most fleeting, expertise authority is the most changeable, and cultural authority is the most frail, yet they all play a part in the authority base from which you will operate.

"And never forget, Redael, authority must be used to serve those who grant it."

"I'll remember, Winning Wizard. I'll remember," Redael asserted.

Confronting Conflict Confidently

"IT PROBABLY WON'T COME AS a surprise to you, Redael," said Winning Wizard, "that all organizations experience conflict. The trick is to make conflict constructive, not destructive."

"Holy cow, Winning Wizard, I thought conflict, by its very nature, was destructive and detrimental to an organization. I would think it could be ruinous!" exclaimed Redael.

"It's true, many organizations let it get out of hand, and it results in a lot of wasted energy and turmoil," Winning Wizard extolled, "but let me tell you a little about conflict so you can confront it with confidence.

"All organizational conflicts can be attributed to one or a combination of four elements:

1. Organizational goals
2. Organizational means
3. Organizational resources
4. Personalities

"Let's examine them one by one," said Winning Wizard, somewhat nonchalantly.

1. **Organizational goals** are subject to interpretation, and therefore value

assessments are attached to them by employees. Many organizations spend days, or even weeks, attempting to clearly and concisely articulate their vision statement, their mission statement, and their goals and objectives. Even then, words will mean different things to different people. What does it mean 'to be the leading organization in the field?' Will you target a select market or a mass market? Do you want to be known as an organizational innovator, or do you equate stability with conservatism? Are you referring to financial values, press acclaim, or consumer surveys? You see the point, Redael. Reasonable people can have reasonable disagreements over organizational goals. So, overall, that example is not a very well-expressed vision statement.

2. **Organizational means** are also subject to employee interpretation and value infusion and, accordingly, hold the potential for conflict. Let's assume for a moment that an organization wants to increase its return on shareholders equity from 20% to 25%. How is this to be done? Should they triple the advertising budget; double the sales force; enter a new market; increase their debt; buy back some of their own stock; sell assets and lease them back; expand research and development; strike new relationships with franchisees, distributors, or suppliers; or all of the above? And, if you do increase advertising, as one example, where do you place it—television, radio, direct mail, billboards, the Internet—and in what proportion? Again, the point is obvious, Redael: There is room for reasonable and legitimate disagreement.

3. **Organizational resources** are always limited and scarce, as demand always exceeds supply. When you prepare budget presentations, you'll find this out in short order. Most employees will tell you they could do their jobs better if they had more help—either operations subordinates or staff assistance. This is an easy trap to fall into and leads to empire building. Don't succumb to it or you'll experience overhead overload, and that militates against a lean, streamlined, high-productivity organization. Still, competition for scarce resources is omnipresent and represents a source of conflict.

4. **Individual personality** conflict often arises out of the first three elements but usually occurs when employees emotionalize them. Personality conflict can often be instinctive, prejudicial, nurtured by stereotyping, or based on a neurosis or psychosis of one or more of the employees involved. Irrespective of the

root cause, personality conflict is the most insidious and injurious to the organization and eruptions cannot be tolerated or condoned.

"That's pretty strong stuff, Winning Wizard," Redael said. "How do you deal with it?"

"I better tell you in the form of

THE WIZARD'S WORDS OF MANAGEMENT WISDOM #17

Don't be intimidated by conflict! Manage it to a creative conclusion, encouraging rational interaction with a vibrant spirit, devoid of invective. Watch out for hidden agendas. Open personality conflict has no place in the organization. If personality pyrotechnics can't be corrected, eliminate the cause(s). The positive organizational environment has no room for petulance, egomania, deviousness, or duplicity."

"Whew!" sighed Redael. "This is pretty deep stuff."

The Benefits of Conflict

"**N**OW THAT YOU KNOW, my dear Redael, that you can never allow yourself to be intimidated by conflict, I need to tell you the benefits of conflict," continued Winning Wizard, "and there are benefits, believe it or not."

"That sounds like an oxymoron to me," Redael said. "I've never thought in terms of beneficial conflict."

"Everything is relative, my young friend, so let me give you nine ways in which conflict is indeed beneficial," said Winning Wizard, with one index finger raised and ready to begin.

1. **Conflict serves to maintain group identity and solidify it.** People have a need for group adhesion, and that can be strengthened when the group takes on an identity of its own and it is given a formal or informal designation. People need a group identity as well as an individual identity, and conflict can help confirm that need and secure it. Project teams, task forces, or special units or squads are all examples of this dynamic.

2. **Conflict can serve as a reason for existence and a frustration release.** Groups working to achieve something are not

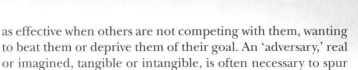

as effective when others are not competing with them, wanting to beat them or deprive them of their goal. An 'adversary,' real or imagined, tangible or intangible, is often necessary to spur the group into action. Frustration releases can also be directed at an adversary rather than at other group members. Adversaries serve a definite purpose. They can be the focus of directed activity and emotional release.

3. **Conflict can reinforce dedication to one's purpose by confirming a determination to succeed.** If something is worth protecting or seeking, conflict increases the desirability of it and the resolve to acquire or secure it.

4. **The closer the relationship between competing groups, the more intense the conflict, the greater the degree of involvement of the participants, and the stronger the desire for total denomination and supremacy.** As an example, the most bitter and acrimonious battles are often those that occur between former friends or partners.

5. **Conflict is a measure of the stability of the relationship between competing groups.** It often becomes ritualistic and ceremonial, as in labor/management negotiations. Such a relationship is beneficial as it's better than an environment where there is no coordination, cooperation, or accepted custom. Some conflict is generated as an expected role or face-saving device as when, for example, an auditor or an inspector must find something 'wrong' or to recommend or else others will think the audit or inspection is not complete.

6. **Open conflict can clear the air if discord and discontent have been seething below the surface.** Once in the open, the resulting emotional catharsis can allow all parties to recognize it, deal with it, and move on. Sometimes, former adversaries become fast friends and former rivals become strong partners.

7. **Conflict tends to unify your adversary, and it's more efficient to engage in battle with one opponent than with several, as your own resources can be used more effectively.** It's better to fight one major adversary than to fight a swarm of smaller adversaries.

8. **The most effective deterrent to internecine conflict is your knowledge of the strength and resources of your adversary, and indications of such may only be able to be determined by probing or by minor skirmishes.** Sometimes rumors are purposely leaked, for example, to identify and observe the reaction of potential adversaries.

9. **Conflict can bring allies to your aid to assist you in your struggle.** Such alliances can prove beneficial in other areas as well as in the area of conflict by building on those relationships. Politics do, in fact, make for strange bedfellows.

"That's amazing, Winning Wizard," exclaimed Redael, tapping a forefinger on the chair. "I can think of examples that fit everything you said, now that I hear your words of wisdom. You are truly wise."

"Don't go overboard, Redael," chastised Winning Wizard. "It's just that I've been around for a long time. Let me sum up my comments on conflict as

THE WIZARD'S WORDS OF MANAGEMENT WISDOM #18

Certain advantages accrue to every conflict situation. Exploiting those advantages strengthens your position. Since conflict can be managed, it is imperative that you do manage it, otherwise you will become the victim, not the victor."

Organization: The Abstraction

"**L**ET'S PLAY A QUICK word-image association game, Redael. I'll mention a word, and you accept and recognize the first image that comes to your mind as the result of hearing the word. Ready? Here's the word—**organization!**

"Quickly! Think! Let the first image develop," commanded Winning Wizard. "Don't suppress it—express it!"

"**Organization!**" said Redael.

"Well, the obvious question that now arises is what was the image you brought to your mind as the result of the word 'organization.' I'll submit that the chances are 9 out of 10 that you let an incorrect, inaccurate, or ill-defined image seep through. Why? Because chances are you are used to thinking in terms of the tangible, the concrete, and the specific, and not the abstract.

"You may have thought of a building, a physical structure of brick and mortar, wood, or glass; offices; or the outside of an imposing edifice. If so, you equate an organization with an institution.

"You may have thought of a diagram, commonly called an organization chart, with boxes and lines in some sort of configurative circuitry.

"You may have thought of a mass of people, either in a collective body or segregated by boundaries of some sort, such as walls, partitions, or lattice work.

"Or, perhaps, you thought of a particular entity, the place where you work, an office building, a school, hospital, or other location that has specific meaning for you.

"It's a normal reaction to think of an 'organization' in those terms, Redael, so don't be unnerved by what I'm going to say," said Winning Wizard patronizingly. "In a real sense an organization is at once all of these elements, and at the risk of adding to the confusion I'll offer the following: An organization is a system of interrelationships between or among two or more persons engaged in the pursuit of a common established goal. An organization is intangible in reality. It depends on people, indeed it is people, but it is people working in a defined, explicitly or implicitly, relationship with each other. What's my point? Just this—if you are going to be a successful manager, you've got to think of an organization not as a tangible entity but as an intangible system of interaction, transactions, and professional relationships.

"All organizations rely basically on two elements in order to succeed: **planning** and **execution**. You may read or hear what others have said are the elements of management. The Frenchman Fayol, for example, coined the acronym POSDCORB, which identified *p*lanning, *o*rganizing, *s*taffing, *d*irecting, *co*ntrolling, *r*eviewing, and *b*udgeting as the spectrum of management. Other management buffs have either elaborated on or abbreviated this list, but it still all comes down to planning and execution. These two activities give rise to four possibilities.

1. Good planning and good execution
2. Good planning and poor execution
3. Poor planning and good execution
4. Poor planning and poor execution

"Number one is the exception to the rule, and number four, regrettably, is becoming increasingly common. That leaves two and three. Which is preferable? Well, here are

The Wizard's Words of Management Wisdom #19

A poor plan well executed is always superior to a good plan poorly executed.

"Why, Redael? It's simple. Planning is done by a few, but execution is accomplished by many. If many people are working in proper execution sequence, it's more efficient to refine the planning or change the planners. A smoothly functioning organization can change direction far more easily than can an uncoordinated organization. Baseball managers and football coaches get fired if the team doesn't win. The team doesn't get fired. They need to get fired up!"

"You are right on, Winning Wizard," marveled Redael, "I have never before thought of an organization as a system of relationships between and among people. I guess I never gave it much thought at all, to tell the truth."

"That's OK, Redael. You are right at the point you should be in your managerial development. That's the benefit of having conversations such as this, so we can expand our intellectual horizons and rise to greater levels of achievement, service, and responsibility," Winning Wizard lectured, feeling good that a new horizon had been opened to the young trainee.

"By the way, Redael, also remember

The Wizard's Words of Management Wisdom #20

Most people think in concrete terms, as opposed to abstract terms, most of the time. Don't get stuck in concrete."

Organizational Values

"**A**S YOU GAIN MORE EXPERIENCE, Redael, you will understand that organizations possess and evoke values just as people do," mused Winning Wizard. "That should not surprise you, since, remembering that an organization is a network of people, organizational values are usually a reflection of the personal values of the founder or the chief executive. I have found it best to match an individual with an organization that has the same values as the individual, as that usually results in good personal/organization 'chemistry.' A mismatch of values between the organization and the individual usually does not serve either well in terms of sustaining a long-term relationship."

"I've never really realized organizations could have values, Winning Wizard. I've just thought of them as being institutionally sterile," confessed Redael. "What should I look for?"

"Let me give you some examples, Redael, and you'll see the point," countered Winning Wizard.

> *1.* **Competition–Compassion.** Some organizations are known for their fierce, intense, hyper-aggressive competitive instincts and techniques. They stop at virtually **nothing** to expand their share

of the market, win the account, pirate personnel, play accounting games to hype the market price of their shares, stop just
short of misrepresentation in their advertising, deride competitors through comparative advertising, and so on. Yet in
these same organizations, the instinct and emotionalism of
compassion also exists. For example, many organizations have
developed policies concerning donations and contributions to
public works projects, educational programs, and charities.

In this sense, these firms are outstanding corporate citizens.
What is often muddled, however, is the purpose for which the
'gift-giving benefit program' is used. Is it an element of an
overall marketing strategy, a public relations tool, a sales promotion technique, a publicity stunt, a 'we can afford it this
year' impulse, or an act of contrition? The only economic jus-
tification for such gift programs is that the long-term benefit
of the program will be greater, directly or indirectly, than its
short-term cost. The social benefit is that society is enriched by
such largesse, which adds to the quality of life, which, in turn,
benefits the organization.

2. **Equality–Equity.** In Human Resources administration, for
   example, standards and practices must be developed and
   maintained to ensure equal and objective application to, and
   treatment of, **all** employees. In evaluating performance, however, based on differences in abilities, interests, aptitudes, and
   overall contributions to organizational goals, people on the
   same organizational level must be differentiated. The task is
   not to treat each employee equally, but to differentiate
   employees so that each can be treated equitably. It's absolutely
   necessary to be 'fair' to each employee, but fairness is an intangible, and if a fair judgment is based on an intangible circumstance, the decision is fraught with the potential for
   misinterpretation. How many hours have you spent with dis-
   traught employees who misperceived or rejected outright your
   'fairness' in handling their situation? The point is that equality of opportunity is not synonymous with, nor does it mandate
   equality of, distribution of rewards because performance and
   effort are rarely identical. Only rarely can you get away from
   subjectivity when you are dealing with people.

3. **Conformity–Creativity.** There are decided benefits to stan-
   dardizing the organizational behavior of employees. If you
   train well, for example, a constancy of image, impact, level,
   and quality of product and/or service is the end result. But to

what extent does such mental and behavioral control inhibit creativity, which also has its benefits, and, if allowed to function unfettered, could be tremendously beneficial to the organization? I recognize that you can counter on this point, Redael, by stating that you will allow for creativity within the broad boundaries of conformity, through informal meetings with employees, suggestion systems, brainstorming sessions, retreats, and so on, along the conform–create dimension. There is a difference between conformity and puppetry, just as there is between creativity and fantasy.

4. **Centralization–Decentralization.** Certain economies of scale, internal efficiency, fingertip control, and purchasing power often accompany centralized authority. Unfortunately, in some instances, so do inconsistency, mistrust, delay, misunderstanding, lack of confidence in headquarters by the field force, and demoralization. The advantages and disadvantages with centralization are often reversed with the advent of decentralization. On rare occasions, it's possible to have the best of both worlds. For example, in cash management, you can centralize collections but decentralize disbursements. The basic question is whether there is a concentration of authority or a distribution of authority.

"There are many other organizational value comparisons that I could mention, Redael. Where is the balance between innovation of a new concept and imitation—that is, taking someone else's concept—between adoption of a code of ethics, for example, and adaptation, such as a compromise of principle in the vein of 'When in Rome, do as the Romans do'?

"There are no textbook answers to these issues, Redael. You have to look at different organizations and decide what the best 'fit' is for you.

"Well, my friend, where does this leave us with this discussion?" Winning Wizard questioned. "Allow me to set forth

THE WIZARD'S WORDS OF MANAGEMENT WISDOM #21

Most people can make decisions on the basis of facts. A more limited number of people can make decisions on the basis of timely interpretation of facts. The most far-reaching and significant decisions, however, are made on the basis of values."

"Winning Wizard," said a thankful Redael, "I am truly valuing this conversation."

Organizational Competition

"WE NEED TO DISCUSS another organizational dynamic, Redael, as part of your overall understanding," Winning Wizard said, "and that is the subject of intraorganizational competition.

"I suspect you frequently have been in a competitive situation within the various organizations of which you have been a part.

"It probably started when you first realized you were a member of a group. That group could have been a family organization, grade school class, little league team, or whatever, and now you are part of an economic organization.

"A question arises: 'Is competition between and among the group members of an organization good?'

"Your first inclination, Redael, no doubt, is to say that it is, for the very word 'competition' stimulates a reactive emotion within you that gives rise to an inner drive to express and release your own prowess.

"The nation's economy is based on the free enterprise system, in which competition is the model, and we have been conditioned to the suggestion that competition brings out the best.

"But does it? And if it does, does it also bring out the worst?

"Consider a training situation first. A group of trainees are assembled, and the trainer explains, demonstrates, shows aids, coaches, and evaluates the individuals in the group in the performance of the task.

"The trainer then inserts a competitive technique. The first person to finish, considering speed and accuracy, will receive a reward. Or, the last one through will receive a negative reinforcement such as extra work, extra practice, overtime work, or additional assignments. Sound familiar, Redael?" Redael nodded.

"What does this competitive technique really do? It identifies the above-average, average, and below-average trainees. Fine! But it's just possible that the above-average trainee performed well by nature of his or her superior general competence, previous experience, or characteristics peculiar to the training environment, materials, and/or performance time.

"If the trainee has been habitually superior in past activities, and the training exercise is another demonstration of it, that trainee may lose interest, become overconfident, and/or be condescendingly egotistical.

"If the below-average performer has been habitually poor in past activities due to awkwardness, slowness, or whatever, the trainer has set conditions where, once again, this trainee's inferiority is confirmed. The trainee, therefore, condemns herself or himself to a legacy of poor performance, and the possible self-debasement syndrome deepens.

"'Don't keep him or her,' you might say! OK, but bring in the next training group, and if the same competitive technique is used, you'll be turning some away from that group, too. If the organization can afford that type of training 'turn-in turn-out' activity, fine, you'll only keep the superior performers, but for how long? And those you keep may shake out if the same interpersonal competitive techniques are used on the job—which means, Redael, you'd better oil the revolving door.

"Take a second case. Several unit managers are placed in competition with one another; but their track records, markets, locations, and facilities are different. Under such different conditions there is no way that such competition can be conducted equitably.

"I know, Redael, you can cite examples of great turnaround situations, but those are the long shots, and besides, all the variables that happened to blend properly are peculiar to that specific situation.

"By now you may think I'm speaking against competition. No, I'm not. I'm speaking against the misuse of **intraorganizational** competition, which is not to be confused with **interorganizational** competition. What constitutes proper use and misuse?

"My answer is

THE WIZARD'S WORDS OF MANAGEMENT WISDOM #22

Interpersonal competition within an organization should only occur when there is a close commonality of personal competence, experience, resources, environment, goals, and such other variables that will influence the outcome. In all other cases, individual self-competition should be used, matching an individual's present performance with his or her own past performance.

"In this way, the challenge is to better oneself, and you don't match a lightweight against a heavyweight. No one really wins in that case."

"Right on, Winning Wizard. I know exactly whereof you speak. I've experienced both types of competition," agreed Redael. "That's a great point: Self-competition can lead to self-improvement. I'll always remember that."

Organizational
Recreation

"ORGANIZATIONAL LIFE, REDAEL, is more than just the time you consider to be your 'work hours,'" Winning Wizard noted. "You become identified with your organization, and it's with you 24 hours a day. Let's talk about the appropriate role for a leader in an organizational recreational setting.

"In most organizations, occasions arise in which employees have an opportunity to 'let their hair down.' Such situations usually involve a company-sponsored social event celebrating a holiday period or marked business peak, milestone, or anniversary. Most industrial psychologists, human resource experts, and business consultants advocate such festivities for the creation or maintenance of group spirit, pride, morale, and bonding for the overall well-being of the firm. That's all well and good, but let's move from this 'macro' approach to the 'micro' approach. Specifically, what is the leader's role in terms of what the leader should do, and not do, at company social outings? We'll take one example to illustrate the point, Redael, but realize you can generalize the concept.

"You are at a company-sponsored picnic and can participate in a pick-up softball game, act as the bartender, sit in on a poker game, engage in informal conversation by 'mixing,' or cook the steaks, franks, etc. You are not a good softball player or card player, but you have played both in other settings in the past. What would, or should, you do, given these three assumptions?

1. Your organizational position is higher than any other person in attendance.

2. You attend the function because not attending without a **real** reason could be misunderstood as unpardonable aloofness.

3. You don't purposely come so late as to 'escape' these activities.

"The pros, cons, and evaluations follow:

1. **Play Softball.** You could be considered as a 'regular' person and real team participant both on and off duty. This is the only possible organizational benefit. A personal benefit would be the exercise. Potential disadvantages could be a subversive attempt to make you look foolish by forcing errors and over-extending the physical aspect by sliding, tripping, causing a collision, or causing minor injury, which would dampen the game and could be evident when you are back in the office. Others might cater to you since you are not a good player, thereby offering special privileges in a competitive circumstance, which would magnify your inability as a player. My evaluation, Redael, is *don't play a sport unless you're good at it.*

2. **Be the Bartender.** The advantage is that this role places you in a control position, which is one aspect of your management responsibilities. Simultaneously, it's a disadvantage since the substance—liquor, wine, or beer—can be behavior changing, and a perception can be advanced that you stationed yourself there to make moral judgments or informal professional evaluations. Irrespective of your intentions, others might think you were watching and counting, which would nullify group enjoyment. If anyone did over-indulge and become abusive or raucous, it would be embarrassing to you as the 'controller.' Furthermore, if someone fell victim to over-consumption, a guilt feeling could extend to and damage the working relationship. My evaluation, Redael, is *don't be the bartender.* The only exceptions are if the activity is held in your home or at the organizational location.

3. **Play Poker.** The sole organizational advantage is to be perceived as a 'regular' person, but this situation is fraught with danger. Your economic status may open you to charges of 'buy-

ing a pot.' Cards can also lead to a test of wills of the participants where emotionalism overruns objectivity and good sense. Great gains or losses on the part of one or more participants could have serious consequences on working relationships. Pot or raise limits don't restrict the psychological relationships, only the economic ones. Participants could also spot your inclination to take risks or avoid risks, which can carry over to your professional life. My evaluation, Redael, is *do not play poker with subordinates.*

4. **Mix Informally and Converse.** The advantage is that this innocuous activity holds little potential for detrimental effects. It allows you to mingle with others in a nonorganizational environment. You don't run any risk of appearing foolish, athletically so, or becoming an unspoken object of derision. The main disadvantage is that other participants may be unduly inhibited, expecting you to do something in the social situation that would serve to assert and confirm your organizational authority. This activity allows you to leave early with minimum disruption. As a personal note, you'll need a high tolerance for small talk—don't get trapped by one subordinate who wants to get something off his or her chest, and be careful of forming your own clique with your closest associates. My evaluation, Redael, is that *overall, this is one of two good choices of those offered,* but be sure you touch bases for a 'hello' to everybody. No omissions.

5. **Be the Cook.** This depends on the prior planning of the activity. This role may have already been assigned. If not, there are many advantages to your undertaking it. It places you in a 'controller's' position, but you're dealing with a food substance rather than a behavior-changing substance. The party's focus at some time will shift to food, and since the organizational focus is on you in the organizational environment, it's reinforcing to have this type of focus on you in the social environment. Gluttony on a sometime basis is not as stigma attracting as inebriation on a sometime basis. Furthermore, this type of activity is easily delegated after the 'rush,' and, barring culinary disaster, you will be the recipient of appreciative compliments. Furthermore, you fulfill the expectations of many others in this 'take charge' function, and the transfer of responsibility acceptance from an organizational scene to a social scene is on an equal plane. The disadvantages are personal, only being some degree of inconvenience, perhaps. My

evaluation, Redael, is *that if the need and opportunity are there, cook the food.*

"Allow me to summarize with

THE WIZARD'S WORDS OF MANAGEMENT WISDOM #23

Ensure the nonbusiness activities you engage in with organizational subordinates informally reinforce established formal organizational working relationships. There is a carry-over effect."

"It really is true, isn't it, Winning Wizard, that everything I do, in all aspects of my life, has some bearing on my position," said Redael, having received a new insight.

"Yes, Redael, it is true," Winning Wizard remarked. "You can't divorce segments of your life from one another over the long run."

Organizational Physics

"I HAVE FOUND IT QUITE INTERESTING, Redael, that there are some parallels that can be drawn between the world of science and the world of management," Winning Wizard expounded with a wry smile. "If you are up to it, I'll give you some examples."

"Sure thing, Winning Wizard. I've never thought about that before either, so I'm taking in everything that you say," said the eager student.

"Good!" replied the mentor. "I'll tell you the scientific principle, then I'll give you my counterpart management principle."

"I'm ready," Redael replied.

"OK. Here we go!" said Winning Wizard.

> *1.* Essentially, Newton's first law of gravity is 'What goes up must come down!' So here are

THE WIZARD'S WORDS OF MANAGEMENT WISDOM #24

One who goes up must stay up — or go out!

2. Another of Newton's laws basically states, 'A body at rest tends to remain at rest. A body in motion tends to remain in motion.'

THE WIZARD'S WORDS OF MANAGEMENT WISDOM #25

If you want something done, give the assignment to a busy person.

3. Archimedes studied fluids and determined essentially that 'any body, either wholly or partially submerged in a fluid, is buoyed up by a force equal to the weight of the fluid displaced.'

THE WIZARD'S WORDS OF MANAGEMENT WISDOM #26

Any manager, either wholly or partially submerged in a fluid—or by a fluid—eventually is going to encounter a pulled plug!

4. Newton's third law states fundamentally that 'if one body, A, exerts a force on another body, B, then B must exert an equal and opposite force on A.'

THE WIZARD'S WORDS OF MANAGEMENT WISDOM #27

Leadership is not unidirectional. It is a process of directed activity that must be met in an equal and complementary measure of acceptance of that direction by subordinates.

5. The Englishman Hooke found that 'the deformation of a solid body is proportional to the force acting on it.'

THE WIZARD'S WORDS OF MANAGEMENT WISDOM #28

The formation and development of an organization is directly proportional to the commitment given to it.

6. Doppler studied sound and postulated that 'sound will change pitch depending on the movement of the source or the listener.' Think of a train whistle on a moving train or a car horn on a moving car.

THE WIZARD'S WORDS OF MANAGEMENT WISDOM #29

The greater the organizational communication distance, the less you will be heard and regarded.

7. The Frenchman Le Chatelier said, 'Whenever action is taken to change an existing physical system, the system reacts in such a way to oppose such action.'

THE WIZARD'S WORDS OF MANAGEMENT WISDOM #30

Whenever action is taken to change an existing organizational system, the system reacts in such a way to delay that change and alter such change in a manner that most closely resembles the original system.

8. I'm not sure who it was, Redael, who studied light and came up with this principle," confessed Winning Wizard, "but the principle is 'the angle of reflection equals the angle of incidence.'

THE WIZARD'S WORDS OF MANAGEMENT WISDOM #31

Face issues squarely, not obliquely, and make decisions on the basis of facts and values, not emotion or personal relationships.

9. Einstein's theory of relativity eventually states 'absolute true and mathematical time, of itself and from its own nature, flows equally without relation to anything external.'

THE WIZARD'S WORDS OF MANAGEMENT WISDOM #32

Do it right the first time. You may not have a second chance. "

"I'm astonished, Winning Wizard," Redael blushed, feeling overwhelmed again. "Those parallels get to the heart of a lot of organizational dynamics, don't they?"

"Yes, Redael, they do," tutored Winning Wizard. "You can learn more from the different fields of science than just matters that are internal to the discipline."

Taking the Lead

"**T**O BE A SUCCESSFUL EXECUTIVE, Redael, you need to understand the concept of leadership," said Winning Wizard matter-of-factly. "Not many people really understand it, and that's why there is constant attention being drawn to it. There is a lot that needs to be said, so let's get into it now."

"Sure, Winning Wizard," Redael said excitedly. "You have my undivided attention."

Winning Wizard began, "There has never been a universally accepted definition or explanation of **leadership**. There have been several theories advanced as to who a leader is, what a leader is, and what a leader does.

"**Trait theory** has attempted, unsuccessfully, to identify the single physical and/or personality trait, or blend of traits, that identifies a leader. Nothing has been concluded definitively.

"**Role theory** has focused insufficiently on the functions of the leader—that is, does the leader establish goals or implement means to reach goals, or, if both, in what proportion? Does the leader revise goals or intensify existing goals and/or means? Role theory has never really distinguished between an administrator, a manager, a policy maker, an executor, and a leader.

"**Intent theory** analyzes the acts of leaders, in terms of what their motivations are as manifested by their actions. Are they group oriented, so they spend time establishing and strengthening the interpersonal relations of group members—that is, group maintenance and group hygiene, or are they primarily interested in coaxing the group to accomplish its objectives, focusing on group achievement?

"Most recently, **plural leadership theory** has suggested that no one person can exert all of the forces necessary to attain a desired result in a group context and that leadership is shared to some extent among all the members of the group. This, perhaps, tends to cloud the question rather than clarify it.

"Although it is complex, Redael, there are some things we can say with certainty about leadership.

1. Leadership resides in a person. Machines and signs can't lead; they can direct, but inanimate objects do not lead.

2. Leadership is easier to detect than it is to define. We can recognize it when we see it, but we have difficulty analyzing it and articulating it.

3. Leadership should not be confused with positionship. A position holder is not necessarily a leader. A position holder can be a tyrant, manipulator, resource controller, dictator, and the like, yet that person won't be considered a leader.

4. A leader must have a following of one or more people. Leaders lead *people*. Cattle herders or sheep herders, *per se*, are not leaders.

5. Leadership is fluid and changeable, depending on the person, the group, and the situation.

6. The group must accept freely the efforts of the leader for leadership to occur.

7. The situation must require a leadership act for leadership to occur. Leaders have to *do* something. Leadership is active, not passive.

"Here is my definition of leadership," opined Winning Wizard, "which serves as

THE WIZARD'S WORDS OF MANAGEMENT WISDOM #33

Leadership is the art of seeking attainment of organizational goals through working with, over, and/or under other people by securing their willing cooperative efforts while simultaneously satisfying individual and group personal and professional developmental needs."

"Oh, I know, Redael, you can find fault with this, but before you do, consider the following:

1. Leadership is an art, not a science. It emanates from within the person rather than existing in objective reality.

2. A leader seeks attainment and keeps seeking it. Even when goals are reached, new goals are set and the effective leader continues striving on behalf of the group.

3. The leader works with, over, and/or under other people. A leader does not always have the top position; as a subordinate, a person can be the unmistaken leader of the group. The leader can work with others as a first among equals or over others. Leadership and positionship do not always coincide.

4. 'Willing cooperative efforts' involve the follower's free will and efforts with no coercive element existing.

5. **Individual** personal and professional needs must be satisfied. Personal needs are physiologic needs—safety and security, belonging, esteem, self-actualization, and knowing and understanding—and esthetic needs, which Abraham Maslow categorized. Professional needs are to communicate, to strive to accomplish, and to gain recognition, among others.

6. **Group** personal and professional needs must be satisfied. Groups have the same personal needs as individuals but on a collective basis. They also have professional needs such as the need for group identification, a productive environment in which to function, and a sense of achievement.

"A leader, Redael, must be able to pull from the front, push from the rear, and nudge from the side. Mistakes will occur. You must accept that occurrence, but you should not tolerate it. Leaders make sure that any mistakes that are made are only made once.

"And at this point, Redael," Winning Wizard counseled, "realize that leaders make the uncommon common, the difficult easy, the unthinkable thinkable, and the inactionable actionable. They also motivate, delegate, empower, and inspire followers."

"That's pretty overwhelming, Winning Wizard," said Redael, looking a bit overwhelmed. "I hope I can rise to that as circumstances warrant!"

"You can, Redael, you can," assured Winning Wizard, "but no one said it would be easy."

Leadership Traits

"NOW IT IS TRUE, REDAEL, that no single combination of traits has ever been identified that guarantees that a person will be a leader, with every type of group, in every kind of situation," said Winning Wizard ruefully. "Life, and leadership, are not that simple."

"There must be some evidence of leadership traits that have proved successful, isn't there?" quizzed Redael.

"Yes, that's true. Some traits have been identified that are characteristic of leaders, but it's not foolproof, and the absence of one, or the presence of some other, is not any guarantee. Nonetheless, Redael, it is instructive to know what they are so you can nurture them," said Winning Wizard. "Here they are.

1. **Intelligence.** Successful leaders possess, and are perceived by group members to possess, an elevated degree of intelligence relative to the average intelligence of the group. Group perceptions often confuse 'possession of knowledge' with innate intelligence, however. Further, excessively superior intelligence on the part of a 'leader' can result in ostracism, subterfuge, or bemusement by the group. It can

work against you, but, generally, demonstrated intelligence is an absolute requirement for organizational success.

2. **Desire for Excellence.** Successful people evidence a constant pursuit of perfection, a striving to reach beyond the ordinary to a level of astonishing achievement. This trait often manifests itself through a wide grasp of, and attention to, detail. Frequently, this detail consciousness is perceived as 'pickiness' by less perceptive subordinates unless the broader foundations of personal and professional competence have been laid firmly by the leader and have been demonstrated in the past.

3. **Conscientiousness.** This is the conscious acceptance of the responsibility of the position, an understanding of one's role in the organization, and the thoughtful use of authority. One should not be trapped by the 'I wouldn't ask you to do anything I wouldn't do myself' syndrome. One person has only so much of a mental/physical range. It varies. The conscientious executive will **delegate** in good faith and won't relegate simply out of mental/physical necessity. Leaders are perceived to, and in fact do, put in more hours, and more into the hours, than the average group member, which is the tangible and visible evidence of the executive's acceptance, understanding, and commitment to the role and to the organization.

4. **Diligence.** Fierce tenacity to the accomplishment of objectives, both short term and long term, is a characteristic of the successful leader. The 'stick-to-itiveness' exhibited by the leader's organizational attention span precludes wanton dissipation of resources by 'riding off in all directions at once.' Leaders also recognize weak spots and losses earlier than the average group member does and are not timid in altering resources or reshaping objectives in light of those circumstances.

5. **High Upward Mobility Drive.** This has been identified to exist at the personal level, versus the organizational context, in successful leaders. They seek to be known as people of impact, influence, and presence. They view this as a means of accumulating increased amounts of responsibility channeled to defined or created organizational goals. They **accept praise and adulation but are not affected by it** except as a reinforcer of the mobility drive.

6. **Self-confidence.** Leaders have tremendous faith in their own abilities and their own judgment. They look to their own developed standards as a basis for their actions and are not swayed by 'bandwagon psychology' or the 'go along to get along' precept. They are independent of, but not removed

from, others. They rely on good eye contact and exhibit a strength of honesty, integrity, and the 'habit of command.' They are not befuddled by new situations; rather, they handle them directly and adeptly.

7. **Extroversion.** Group members perceive successful executives as mixing and mingling among them freely with no self-consciousness. Leaders are active people, finding reward and enjoyment in personal interaction, and contribute measurably to the facilitation of both professional and social communication interchange. Successful executives who have 'risen from the ranks' exude an air that sets them apart from—not necessarily above—the group of which they were once a member.

8. **Communication Capability.** This involves two elements. First, the successful leader is one who can quickly and accurately view and summarize group thinking and sentiments. Second, the leader is an individual who possesses more information than the average group member. Often this is a function of the communication flow coming into the position, from which the incumbent benefits, who then is the communications receiver, coordinator, filter, synthesizer, and distributor. A person holding such a position is at an advantage compared to those who have only a piece of the total picture. One who can distill a mélange of facts and feelings, and summarize them in a cogent, articulate manner without demeaning their complexity, is in command of the situation.

9. **Humor.** Leaders have been measured and found to possess a constructive sense of humor. They have the ability to laugh at themselves and do not feel threatened by the injection of humor that is in proper perspective, occasion, and tone in the organizational context. They are not intense to the point of no return, retaining the ability to step back from the situation and assess it with a fresh pair of eyes, sparkling with a trace of excitement and levity.

10. **Team Player.** The group's perception of a leader is culturally based to some extent. The strong leader is expected to represent, through personification, action, and vocalization, the values and goals of the group. To this degree, the leader is the group's 'good example' and is, to all outside the group, the symbol and substance for which it stands. The leader is one of the group but is a 'first among equals.' The leader is rarely perceived as manipulative of people, only of inanimate resources, and maintains constant attention and reference to the group's goals.

11. **Planning.** Leaders spend considerable time planning. Successful executives plan for both the short range and long range, continually relating one such element to the other. The leader simultaneously must be short-sighted and far-sighted, must possess foresight as well as hindsight, and must have a molar view as well as a molecular view. Planning gives purpose to the organization. Leaders know, and are perceived to know, where they are taking the organization.

12. **Decisiveness.** Leaders are decisive in the actions they take. They are not encumbered by self-doubt and do not reflect on regrets in hindsight. They know the hardest decisions of all are 'people decisions.' It does not mean they act quickly, act on inadequate information, or are rigid once committed to a course of action, if subsequent events change. It does mean they set the direction and then move toward it, making course corrections as necessary.

"This list is not exhaustive, Redael. It is merely representative of what a lot of research has determined, as to the traits possessed by leaders generally conceded to be successful executives."

"There is a lot of substance to all that, Winning Wizard," said Redael, with a degree of wonderment. "I really need to digest all of it."

"Yes, Redael," responded Winning Wizard, "but I have faith that you can do it. Let me summarize these thoughts as

THE WIZARD'S WORDS OF MANAGEMENT WISDOM #34

The successful executive has established an emotional equivalency between organizational accomplishment and personal growth, has a sense of unfulfillment with regard to what remains to be accomplished, and possesses the resources and authority to effect greater accomplishment."

Leadership Qualities

"SINCE WE HAVE DISCUSSED leadership traits, Redael, we should now move to examining leadership qualities," said Winning Wizard, somewhat didactically. "Allow me to set the stage, and then we'll address some essential qualities necessary for success.

"Success in the executive managerial ranks rests on the elements of the leader, the group, and the situation in interaction with one another. The group and the situation are often fluid—emerging, converging, diverging, resurging—in a cyclical and, hopefully, progressive pattern. The leader must recognize these stages of group and situation dynamics and bring skill, talent, and capabilities to bear on them. This is not to say the leader must be a chameleon, changing colors as it were depending on one's mood. It does mean that a leader must call from the personal innermost resources that element or combination of elements in just the right proportion, and with just the right degree of intensity, to draw the utmost from the group as it interfaces with the situation to achieve organizational goals.

"Earlier we identified some key traits that successful leaders possess. We now go beyond the identification to determine what belief and behavior patterns successful leaders exhibit in their relations with others.

"Truly successful leaders are generous people, not necessarily in the financial sense but in the recognition that their talents, while residing in their person, in fact belong to the organizations they serve. Their contributions and satisfactions take force not in their giving or receiving, but in the activating, for they know that it is through activity that expression and creativity give rise to organizational and personal development. In that sense, they know it is nice to give and receive, but it is better to activate.

"The successful leader believes that success comes from competition, not largesse nor monopoly, and that competition does not, in the total sense, involve the destruction of competitors, but involves the leader's fortification and resolve, which in turn is stimulating and developmental to the organization.

"There is no shrinking from competition or challenges; rather, there is a hard-nosed resolve to conquer it.

"The successful leader knows that success is the mastery of a situation but that success is accompanied, however slightly, by a fear of failure, based on a possible change in the situation or a change in society's values as to what was once desirable becoming undesirable. Since we cannot conquer unpredictability, we are forced to live with it. The leader does so, however, with rationality, poise, professionalism, a secure confidence, an aura of courage, and a buoyancy of spirit.

"Successful leaders have a mature appreciation of the complexity of the decisions they make, relative to the uncomplicated minds they may have possessed earlier in their careers, when matters were 'simpler' and the 'right' decisions seemed ever so much more obvious. Yet, they do not require a 'crutch' to 'escape' complexity; rather, they find enjoyment and solace in the analysis of the very factors that go into the decision-making process.

"Leaders condense their organizational leadership roles into a relatively few fundamental operating notions. They are people of recognized intellectual capability, and although they are detail conscious, they are not detail confined. They match their overview with their purview and, consequently, are objects of esteem and respect by their subordinates.

"The successful leader possesses a guarded trust of others, having experienced both the joy of subordinates working to and beyond their capability and disappointment due to the tragedy and treachery of human failings in others. The organization is viewed neither as a corporate jungle nor a corporate infirmary but as an economic and social system of which the leader is a part and for which the leader has full responsibility.

"Successful leaders are adept at seeing an interconnectedness to events that the average person sees as isolated, unrelated incidents. Consequently, they have a mental framework for decision-making purposes that simultaneously is expansive and precise. Their ability to see and draw relationships among these things that affect their organizations provides them with the 'sixth sense' on which they can take action. They think both strategically and tactically.

"So, Redael, let me conclude this portion of our discussion with

THE WIZARD'S WORDS OF MANAGEMENT WISDOM #35

The successful leader demands and receives a sharp performance edge from the organization, which gives it a competitive edge, frequently becoming a cutting edge, resulting in a winning edge.

"That's right, Redael, it's good to be on edge," said Winning Wizard, with eyes twinkling.

Leadership Style: The Imperial Emperor/Empress

CHAPTER

"WELL, REDAEL, LET'S GET PRACTICAL at this point and talk about leadership styles," Winning Wizard remarked, somewhat off-handedly. "There are a lot of styles that have a lot of names, but I've witnessed three fundamental approaches to the practice of leadership. We'll discuss each of them, but I'll start with the 'Imperial Emperor' or 'Empress.' I'll exaggerate a little, perhaps, to emphasize the points, but a lot of people really are imperial in large part, irrespective of whether they admit to it. Let's take a peek at their mindset.

1. **Employees are lazy—they don't want to lead, they must be led.** You employees fall into the same category as cattle. You're meek, mild, timid, and lack direction and intelligence, and you would follow anyone who promised you comfort, convenience, and security. You don't know the meaning of leadership, and, if you did, you wouldn't want it. You are indolent, stupid, devious, and self-indulgent. That's why control systems and security systems are necessary. As good fortune for you, I am here to provide you with leadership and direction. I'll take care of it—it's my management burden. I'll organize and direct things, just do as I say. I'll even

help you organize and straighten out your personal life, since you're most likely incapable of that, too. That's why we have a credit union, or I make personal loans to you, and call my contacts when you get into trouble.

2. **Might is right.** I'm more powerful than you are and don't you ever forget it. Don't ever cross me. I've got more money than you do, I'm smarter than you are, and I could crush you if I wanted to. I have more and better political, economic, and social contacts than you can ever hope to have, and, if you do cross me, I'll see to it you never get a job in this city, or this state, as long as you live. You're an adult, and you know on which side of your bread your butter is spread. You're on a limb, and I've got the saw. Now that we understand one another, just do as I say. Don't talk—I don't want to hear it. Just do it and shut up. Discussion closed!

3. **Win at any cost.** Most of you misguided souls have heard and believe that human values, principles, and standards exist in organizations. I've never heard such garbage in all my life. You better believe that the only things in life that have 'values, principles, and standards' are the budget and the bottom line. Survival of the fittest applies to organizations as the law of this jungle. It's the big green that counts, and, if I have to stomp on others to get it, I will. Nothing personal, but I'll stomp so hard I won't be pestered again. I may have to lie, cheat, swindle, stab others in the back, break my word, bribe, evade taxes, shade things, and slander. My regret will be if others do it to me before I do it to them. Don't feel shocked—this is not peculiar to me. Look at other organizations, and you'll see the same thing.

4. **Fear is my motivator.** When I walk in, I want you to stand up, bow your head, and lower your eyes. When I say jump, you'd better ask 'how high?'. I don't want to hear anything negative and, if I even get a hint that you resist what I tell you, we'll color you gone. I'm ultimately the one who hired you, and I'm the one who can fire you. After all, there are certain and definite advantages to dismissing people from time to time. If you don't believe me, try me. What's that? You want to try me?

5. **Act precipitously, and keep employees in a state of confusion.** I go away for a few days and when I come back, this place looks like a nuclear meltdown. What did you do, all take vacations or did you just party all the time? I guess the old bromide proves true—when the cat's away, the mice will play. Well, the top cat

is back and I'm docking your pay, and some of you won't be here next week. Don't expect any time off from now on. I try to be fair and you take advantage of me. We're going to have to review our human resources policies, I can see that. Why do I have to be surrounded by such incompetency?

6. **Retain all credit for positive events.** We've had a good year this year—thanks to my leadership, the many hours I've put in, and the foresight I've displayed. Our organization has grown, obviously as the result of my acumen and performance. Someone once said that no one is indispensable. Don't believe it, I am. I had my picture in all the media representing you. Never mind what the reports said. Is it my fault commoners don't recognize genius when I'm with them? We achieved some record highs this year, personnel turnover, complaints, and threatening phone calls. That was your fault. I don't know what this world is coming to!

7. **Escape adversity!** Of course, there are some things that haven't gone very well this year, but it wasn't *my* fault. If you employees had just done what I told you, everything would have been all right. Why do I always have to come into the middle of things and do it for you? The IRS says there are some irregularities in our books, but I always said you could never trust accountants. They said I directed them to make some questionable entries, but no one has it in writing. Besides, I have a memo that I wrote to the file on the matter at the time of our conversation and the memo says the opposite of what is alleged. By the way, I've just put Percy here in charge of operations, and he told me he was going to trim the workforce by 25%. Didn't you, Percy? Speak up, Percy.

8. **Glamorize tokenism.** All in all, we came out pretty well this year. Yes, it was tough, but I did it. As an expression of my appreciation to you, I want you to know that I'm raising your salaries $1 per week. That annualizes out to $52 per year. We'll also take the locks off the restroom doors for an additional 5 minutes in both the morning and the afternoon for your convenience. I've called a press conference to announce these groundbreaking measures to the media.

9. **Create chaos to reinforce power and authority.** We're going to be making some changes around here. I'm not at liberty to say what they are, but you'll find out soon. Then we'll see what you're made of. Also, that vacation schedule I approved for everyone last week, I had to throw it out. I'll make the vacation

assignments. That way you won't have to worry about submitting a request. And in 15 minutes, we're going to shut down for 30 days for some interior renovation.

"Of course, Redael, the Imperial Emperor or Empress leaders are not as blatant as I've portrayed here. They are much more subtle and clever in dealing with others. Yet, their behavior, and what is said from time to time, as well as how it is said, gives clues to their management style. Let me express

THE WIZARD'S WORDS OF MANAGEMENT WISDOM #36

The imperial style is effective when the group is comprised of nonvoluntary participants, with little or loose relationships between and among group members, and when the group is heterogeneous in character or is comprised of people who are conditioned, used to, and comfortable in a power relationship. It is also effective when the situation is one of emergency or crisis. Under any other conditions, in terms of management style, the imperial emperor/empress needs a new set of clothes."

"OK, Winning Wizard, I've seen those types of leaders before," Redael lamented. "It creates a strident environment."

Leadership Style: Angels

CHAPTER

"WE HAVE SEEN, REDAEL, that the imperial leadership style, except in unusual circumstances, is a repressive, power-based approach to managing people," said Winning Wizard with a firm and forceful voice. "Now we need to discuss another style of leadership that, in my experience, most young people try to adopt—until they become scarred by experience. I call it the angelic approach."

"Well, Winning Wizard, I don't think of myself as being imperial, but I have seen a lot of what you have described. I'll try not to let myself fall into that pattern," said Redael with resolve. "But I'm intrigued by the angelic style. I'm ready to hear about it."

"OK, Redael, let me describe organizational angels to you, exaggerating a bit, once again, to illustrate the point," said Winning Wizard with a wry smile.

1. **Employees can be self-directed.** I'm very fortunate you employees decided to work here, and I'm thankful you decided to come in today. As I let you know by word and action, your maximum development can be achieved by free expression and unsupervised activity. Any supervision on my part would

be restrictive and harassing, and, if I did give you an idea or suggestion, that would be dictatorial and controlling. I have complete faith that you see what needs to be done, and because you seek activity as a natural part of existence, you'll do what needs to be done. I believe that the one who supervises the least supervises best, so I'll stay out of your way. The situation will guide most of your activity, so I won't have to.

2. **Right is might.** I fully subscribe to the 'I'd rather be right than be President' approach to management because righteousness always prevails. We may have some temporary setbacks from time to time because some misguided people will take advantage of our honesty, generosity, and faith in them, but they'll learn the error of their ways. It'll all come out in the wash sooner or later. Things have a way of balancing out. We know we're right in what we do, and that's the only source of strength on which we need to draw. We can remain above the adversarial and confrontational aspects of life. If the IRS says we owe, then we pay. If customers complain about anything, we always give them double their money back or don't charge them.

3. **Rules were made to be broken.** Some organizations have rules and regulations, but we don't need to be encumbered by these things—that's for others. I've never seen a rule yet that wasn't broken, so why have them if you're going to make exceptions? The exceptions just lead to more rules. Regulations are an imposition on one's freedom, and we don't want to have that atmosphere here. We really don't need standards either, since they are artificial. All of us are different anyway, and we can set our own pace. I've heard others say that policies were 'guidelines.' That's a wishy-washy, mealy-mouthed approach to things, and the answers to a lot of tough questions are passed off as 'policy.' That's not going to be the case here.

4. **Organization is a family.** We're just one big happy family in this organization, and I look after each and every one of you with immense personal, as well as professional, interest. That's why I've not said anything to you when you came in late or didn't show up. You don't need me to add to your troubles. I regard you as my family, and I know you look at me in the same light. That's why things are always upbeat and positive in this organization.

5. **Free communication—up, down, and sideways.** We, as management, have nothing to keep from employees, and that's

why I always e-mail everyone in the organization with all letters and memos. Yes, it imposes on a lot of your time, but no one can say you are not informed. I believe in open communication. I even keep all of you informed when we're contemplating major organizational changes—that's participative management, too. I just don't know where the time goes.

6. **All credit goes to others.** We've had a good year this year, and it's all thanks to you. I didn't really have anything to do with it. I just fill a figurehead role here—you ladies and gentlemen are the ones to be congratulated. You're the ones who make things happen here. I'm the luckiest person around to have you working here. You're so good, you leave me with nothing to do. That's the sign of a good manager.

7. **Organizational problems? What organizational problems?** We don't have any problems here. Every once in a while a challenge arises, but no problems exist. Like the time an employee was discovered taking a personal computer out the door on the last day of work. The poor guy just wanted to improve his skills, and that's commendable. It's true we've had some customer complaints about the service they've received, but then again, you can't please everybody. The accountant insists on using those red figures on the operating statement, but you have to admit it makes for a colorful report. Things will work out; don't worry about it. Time will take care of everything, and we'll get it behind us.

8. **Generous to a fault.** I believe in taking care of our people and their personal needs. Gloria broke her 1-inch fingernail typing this morning, and I told her she could take the week off until it grows back again. Our salaries are the highest in the industry. Golly gee, wish I could say the same thing about our productivity. I'm more than fair minded—I'm fair handed. If you're having trouble doing your job, I'll be glad to jump in and do it for you. It's good to get back to basics, anyway, with a hands-on approach.

"I suspect, Redael, that you've known Angels in organizations at one time or another, usually for a short time, though, since they don't survive. But why? They're well-intentioned, have a good attitude, and have a pleasant personality, generally speaking. I'll tell you why! They deal emotionally, not rationally. They look for and often see the depth of matters but not the breadth of matters, thereby blinding their mental perspective and mobility. They have never reconciled the concepts of political and spiritual equality with differences in individual capacities, motivation, and values. They rely on flight rather than fight. They are more sensitive than sensible, prone to self-doubt rather than self-confidence. They often panic easily or are passive to a fault. They unwittingly sacrifice leadership for companionship, recognition for resignation, report for rapport, effect for affect, conclusion for occlusion. They are functioning idealists rather than functioning pragmatists. They absorb problems rather than deal with them. They seek popularity, confusing it with respect. They confuse professional responsibility with a blurred concept of human relations. They can do irreparable harm to an organization by destroying any semblance of planning, organization, authority, or control.

"In short, Redael, always remember

THE WIZARD'S WORDS OF MANAGEMENT WISDOM #37

Don't be a management angel!"

⟳

"Wow," gulped Redael. "I think I do possess some angelic qualities, Winning Wizard, but you are right. I can't be this kind of Angel and hope to lead a successful, productive organization."

Leadership Style:
The Pragmatist

"REDAEL, MY FRIEND, I WILL NOW describe the third basic leadership style found in organizations, that which I call 'the pragmatist,'" said Winning Wizard matter-of-factly.

"Is this leadership style better than the other two?" inquired Redael of the wizened wizard.

"Better is a relative term, Redael, but let me describe a pragmatic leader's style to you, and we can then discuss the relative merits when I conclude," answered Winning Wizard.

1. **Maintains a perceptive analysis and judgment of people.** The pragmatist recognizes that a continuum exists over which to measure the desire of people to seek purposeful activity. The pragmatist is not polarized in the viewing of subordinates as competent—incompetent, lazy—active, sincere—insincere, etc. Pragmatists, rather, are unusually adept at evaluating subordinates and recognizing the gradations that exist on a multidimensional measurement scale. Their judgment of people is not infallible, but they can size others up quickly, being accurate far more often than not. They do not rely on first impressions, and their 'sixth sense' and 'inner eye'

can cut to the core of others with whom they relate. They supplement their beliefs in the original three elements for business success—*location, location, location*—with an equal portion of a second set of three additional important elements for success—*people, people, people*—and a third set of elements—*timing, timing, timing.*

2. **Knows that right is might, but it needs an offense and defense.** There are perceived and actual integrity, honesty, character, and objectivity in the pragmatist's relationships with others. This aura, which is set for the entire organization, is both contagious and pervasive. The pragmatist recognizes that some issues have equally valid 'right' but opposing solutions but pursues that which is best for the organization and is on the 'right side' of the question if not 'right on' the question, in the view of others. The pragmatist's personal and organizational rectitude and righteousness are impenetrable, and the pragmatist does not get drawn into conspiratorial webs with politicians or competitors. The pragmatist knows that the best offense is an immovable defense, and the best defense is an unstoppable offense, to use a football metaphor.

3. **Plays by the rules.** Unlike imperialists, pragmatists will not resort to anything, short of physical survival, to win. Unlike angels, pragmatists know specified objectives and a path to reach them have to be set for the organization to operate effectively and efficiently. There is a personal and professional code of behavior by which they operate and will not violate. They do not lie, cheat, swindle, scandal, libel, bias, evade, bribe, conspire, pander, or vindictively inflict damage on others. They live by the philosophy that they do better to, and more for, others than they expect others to do to them, knowing that in this way they can't lose.

4. **Respect is rooted in attainment.** The pragmatist does not want to be feared, knowing that a fear–hate–insecure organizational environment is counterproductive to organizational and personal development. They do not seek 'love' or popularity because they don't need it, having egos that are developed well beyond that stage. Their moments of satisfaction and fulfillment are predicated on the organization working as smoothly, professionally, and perfectly as is humanly possible. They seek respect for their organization, and its success is what they cherish most in their professional lives.

5. **Communicates effectively.** Pragmatists do not give all information to all subordinates, thereby smothering them in paper-

work, overwhelming them with verbiage, and taking up their time in a welter of meetings. Neither do they shroud themselves in secrecy or mislead others for the purpose of staging a personal power demonstration. Pragmatists provide information and a system for information flow that allows others the knowledge and coordination they require or desire to function expertly in their own capacity. Pragmatists write well, speak articulately, and possess expressive features and gestures.

6. **Shares credit for accomplishments.** The pragmatist is the first to recognize that credit for organizational achievement is due to and attributable to everyone in the organization. Their very attachment to the organization has some influence on the results attained. If not, then the organization is overstaffed. While pragmatists distribute and acknowledge credit commensurate with the contributions of others, they also evaluate continually the performance of subordinates, in the light of changing goals, methods, and the external environment. Pragmatists are also not afraid to make hard decisions when hard decisions are called for.

7. **Accepts the mantle of the office.** Pragmatists do not delegate the responsibility and authority for confronting the less desirable aspects of their role. Nor do they ignore problems and let them fester. They do not shirk responsibilities for honest evaluation; communication of non-optimal results; assessment of sub-par employee performance; and high-level discussions with dissatisfied customers, stockholders, etc. They do more than seek to solve problems. They seek to prevent problems.

"Let me summarize the pragmatist's style with

THE WIZARD'S WORDS OF MANAGEMENT WISDOM #38

1. The pragmatist knows that in every respect, substance is
far more important than appearance.

2. The pragmatist knows that professionalism is contagious
and is therefore the consummate professional."

"Well, it's obvious to me, Winning Wizard, that the pragmatist's leadership style is certainly better than the other two," exclaimed Redael self-assuredly. "There's no question about it."

"Be careful, Redael, not to jump to conclusions too quickly," warned Winning Wizard. "We have yet to talk about groups and situations, and the leader is only one part of that dynamic context. But I can understand why you think as you do at this point. Before we move on, let me give you some erudite advice that I call

THE WIZARD'S WORDS OF MANAGEMENT WISDOM #39

You need to read people and situations as accurately and as quickly as you read books."

Knowledgeable Leaders

"I WANT TO CONCLUDE THE SEVERAL points we've made on the subject of leadership, Redael, with what leaders themselves know about the subject," exclaimed Winning Wizard with an air of finality. "These are the things leaders have inculcated through observation, experience, and their own insight.

1. Leaders know that success comes in cans! It doesn't come in 'can'ts' or 'cannots.' Leaders know things should be done, can be done, and they do them.

2. Leaders know that the measure of a team is not how well the team performs when things are going as planned but how well the team performs when things are not going as planned.

3. Leaders know that it is their attitude, not their aptitude, that determines their altitude in life.

4. Leaders know that the most important investment they will ever make is in their integrity.

5. Leaders know that the most important asset they will ever own is their reputation.

6. Leaders know that the most important expenditure they will ever make is the time they give in service to others.

7. Leaders know that the most important thing they put on when they get up in the morning is their smile.

8. Leaders know that when they are faced with a choice between intelligence and experience, they will choose . . . experience. With intelligence you often get arrogance. With experience you usually get wisdom.

9. Leaders live their lives through a zoom lens, not through a rearview mirror.

10. Leaders open their minds before they open their mouths.

11. Leaders know that small minds talk about people. Great minds talk about ideas.

12. Leaders realize that when they become comfortable, they become vulnerable.

13. Leaders possess a lot of WIT: Whatever It Takes.

14. Leaders know that 'winning' starts with 'beginning.'

15. Leaders know that self-confidence comes from internal mastery. Effectiveness comes from external mastery.

16. Leaders don't let a bad experience make them bitter. They know it makes them better.

17. Leaders know that life is not to be measured in terms of an 'unbeaten season.' They know that there will be times when they may lose, but they'll never allow themselves to be defeated.

18. Leaders know that sustained leadership rests on the four cornerstones of ethics, courage, standards, and performance.

19. Leaders know that 'vision' not only involves eyesight but also involves insight and foresight.

20. Irrespective of title, leaders know that they are CEOs: Competent! Effective! Organized!

21. Leaders don't tolerate mediocrity, for they know mediocrity is a step toward degeneration.

22. Leaders know that their improvement attitude is a daily endeavor.

23. Leaders realize that success is not an individual achievement. Many people participated in it: subordinates, customers, teachers, mentors, coaches, etc.

24. Leaders know there is a difference between positionship and leadership. The former rests on power, and the latter rests on consent.

25. Leaders affect situations in greater measure than they allow situations to affect them.

"Now all of these leadership underpinnings could be their own Winning Wizard's Words of Wisdom, Redael," noted the sage with a look of definite self-assurance. "But let me summarize it all with

THE WIZARD'S WORDS OF MANAGEMENT WISDOM #40

Leaders know leadership rests on a platform of loyalty, excellence, attitude, determination, energy, responsibility, standards, honor, inspiration, and performance. In a single word: It's called leadership."

"I don't know what to say," said a stunned Redael. "Those are the most incisive words I've ever heard on the subject of leadership. I'm going to do more than memorize them. I'm going to live them," Redael vowed.

Groups

"NOW, REDAEL, WE NEED TO TURN our attention to the subject of 'groups,' be they employees, volunteer associations, social gatherings, or whatever," said Winning Wizard, gazing intently at the young protégé.

"OK, Winning Wizard, I'm primed for this discussion," noted Redael, sitting alertly erect. "I want to know everything there is to know about groups and group behavior, for if I am going to be a leader, I want to be an effective leader."

"That's the spirit, Redael," stated Winning Wizard approvingly. "Let's get on with it then.

"A leader, by definition, must have a following, and in the realm of human relationships, followership usually involves groups of people. We need to look at who they are, what they are, what characteristics they possess, and how they should be measured, from an organization's viewpoint. It is a simultaneously complex and intriguing subject.

"Let's get definitions out of the way, recognizing that definitions can vary according to purpose, but realizing the necessity to start from a firm, accepted foundation. A **group** is a collection of two or more people assembled as the result of a perceived need or desire to affiliate with one another to satisfy that need or desire through a personal interrelationship. The needs and desires may or may not be the same for each participant, and the intensity of the need may differ. There does not necessarily need to be continuous visual, written, or audible communication, although it's a rare group that doesn't communicate regularly. The perceived expectation of affiliation of a participant with other group members and the bonding that therefore arises can give rise to group behavior, and it is what separates a 'group' from a set of individuals, a mob, a crowd, or an audience. A **formal group** is an assembly of people activated for an expressed purpose known to the participants. Examples are business organizations, school classes, and so on. An **informal group** is a meeting of people for an unspecified purpose more for the benefit of the participant as an individual than for achievement of a designated goal. Examples are a coffee klatch or pick-up lunch-hour bridge or chess games. Informal groups often evolve into formal groups, and formal groups sometimes deteriorate, in function, if not in title, to informal groups.

"Another analysis that can be made is the voluntary or involuntary nature of the group. A **voluntary group** is one that can be entered and left freely. Examples are associations and political parties. An **involuntary group** is one on which there is limitation as to the ease of entry and departure. The military is an example. Groups can be **elected,** such as a Board of Directors; **selected,** such as corporate committees; **occupationally required** by a license, such as lawyers and CPAs; **honorary,** such as Medal of Honor winners; **exclusive,** such as insurance or real estate, million dollar round tables; or **secretive** (a fifth column). As you can see, Redael, groups can be categorized over several criteria.

"OK, you're now the leader. You've got a group to lead. Have you ever really considered the profile of the group you are leading? Why not? The effectiveness of what you want done will be determined in part through its acceptance by the group. Don't only relate to your people on an individual-by-individual basis without considering group dynamics. Here are some characteristics of groups of which you should be conscious in order to have an optimal relationship.

   1. Size—Is it a small group or a large group? Small groups usually foster frequent and close communication. Seven or fewer people usually define a small group, and more than seven is usually considered a large group.

   2. Stratification—Who is assembled? Is it a sub-group of a larger group? Is it everyone in the organization? Department heads?

One department? Unit managers? The day shift? Remember that status differences between and among group members can lead to status affirmation ploys by higher status group members and inhibition on the part of lower status group members.

3. **Homogeneity/heterogeneity**—What is the degree of similar socially relevant and demographic characteristics of group members, such as socioeconomic status, age, interests, gender, and work experience? Homogeneous groups usually coalesce faster than heterogeneous groups, for better or for worse.

4. **Familiarity**—To what degree is there a mutual acquaintance-ship of group members to one another's personal lives and relationships outside the organization? High group familiarity can lead to a stronger tie to group loyalty than to leader loyalty.

5. **Efficacy**—To what degree is the group efficiently operative in functioning as a unit? Groups that work well together could resent any personnel changes in the group. They can freeze new employees out, for example.

6. **Compatibility**—To what degree is mutual respect, agreeable-ness, and visible cooperation evident among group members, versus contentiousness, one-upmanship, and contempt? Open conflict can be dealt with by the leader more easily than group-protected internal hostility.

7. **Commitment**—What degree of significance does the group hold for its members—intense loyalty, benign neutrality, marginal to hostile participation? Strong group identity can lead to immense achievement by the group, and vice versa.

8. **Accessibility**—With what degree of ease can one be included in the group? Is it open to everyone? Is it an 'inner circle'? Restricted? By invitation? Does it represent an accomplished feat to have 'arrived' as a group member? The higher the standards for group participation, the greater the probability for group achievement.

9. **Control**—To what degree does the group regulate the behavior of its members? What are group expectations and chastisements for absence, tardiness, inappropriate remarks, or attempts at dominance by one member of a subgroup? A leader is often well advised to let the group administer its own control mechanisms rather than to exert the leader's own authority.

10. **Flexibility**—To what degree are the group's activities marked by informal behavior rather than rigid adherence to specific procedures? Casually directed behavior can often lead to greater sustained group accomplishment than specified behavior.

11. **Autonomy**—To what degree does the group act independently of other groups? Does it take assignments from other groups, or does it determine its own activities? An autonomous group will usually achieve at a higher level than a dependent group.

12. **Participation**—What is the level of time and effort participants devote to the group's activity? Does it extend beyond the assigned tasks and time so that group members volunteer extra effort and time to ensure completion of the group's objective?

"Let me sum up our discussion of groups so far, Redael, with

THE WIZARD'S WORDS OF MANAGEMENT WISDOM #41

Any group, the participants of which are in frequent contact with one another, will develop a group personality that is **different from, and more than a composite of,** *the personalities of its members. The group personality will be both a reflection of, and a reaction to, the leader. A designated, or an appointed, leader entering the group's environment must learn to deal with the group personality as well as the personalities of individual members.*

"I know this may appear to be somewhat academic, Redael," apologized Winning Wizard, "but it's important to understand the dynamics that can come into play. Just think back, Redael, how many times you've been surprised at the outcome of a meeting in which you have been a participant. Group factors were at work!"

"That's a lot to remember, Winning Wizard," sighed Redael, feeling slightly overburdened. "I think I need a lot of practice."

"It appears to be a lot when you first look at it, my friend," agreed Winning Wizard, "but you get used to it quite quickly. Think about the groups in which you are already a part. You'll see how easy it is to diagnose them," said the sage. "Analyzing groups is only the first step, however. We now have to look at how these characteristics affect group behavior."

Group Behavior

"WE HAVE JUST CONCLUDED that groups have a personality of their own over and above the combination of personalities of the group members. Now, Redael, we'll discuss some aspects of group behavior, about which a leader should be knowledgeable in order to get the maximum performance out of the group.

1. When first assembled, groups are poised with expectant attention. The dynamics of the first meeting, or the first meeting after a period of time, are crucial to the subsequent performance of the group. At the first meeting, the spirit of the group members is generally high, their minds are fresh, and physical fatigue has not set in. Group members are curious about and anxious to receive or form their own direction. Many a meeting has been 'lost' at its inception due to faulty performance in the opening moments. First impressions are semipermanent impressions in a group setting. Above all else, lead with your strength when first approaching a group.

2. In a group setting, the notion of 'impossibility' is reduced. Part of the group personality syndrome is to mentally or vocally demean the difficulty or impossibility of an assigned or suggested task. Often this

is the result of the bravado of one or more key group members, but just as often it is the reluctance of the group, or any member, to acknowledge a 'can't do' attitude. As group members jockey for recognition and status within the group, consciously or subconsciously, a feeling of 'I/We can do anything—let's get going' often pervades the group. Just as individuals can exceed apparent human limits on occasion, groups can, too. Consequently, group involvement can hype individual effort, which in turn can result in the group's superior performance. Athletic coaches call it 'momentum.' The trick is to maintain **perpetual** momentum.

3. Groups foster a sense of diminished personal responsibility. It is axiomatic to say that the larger the group, the greater any individual member's anonymity. As a result, the general responsibility for group actions is distributed over the members and shared by them, in an equal or predetermined proportioned manner. Thus, a single group member, other than the leader, does not have sole responsibility, which can affect the group's judgment. This is why, every so often, a group will go off 'half-cocked,' whereas if each of the members had been approached individually, the results might not have been the same. The leader is ultimately responsible, of course, but when the group is making decisions, the leader is simply the representative or spokesperson of the group, even though the leader may be perceived to provide direction and channel activity. The elected leader functions foremost as the group's 'shining example.' The selected or designated leader is the focal point of decisions, and most group members will not feel a compelling personal responsibility for them.

4. Unless specifically assigned reporting responsibility, most group members will not premeditate carefully and in total perspective the purpose or desired outcome of the meeting. Group members, usually due to the press of time engaged in their own functioning, will not devote much time to preparation for the group meeting they are about to attend. An exception occurs when a group member has a particular point or program the member wishes to present and have accepted, but even then the member's attention will be devoted to that aspect rather than the total overview of the group's functioning. The group perceives the leader to hold responsibility for coordinating, integrating, and summarizing group direction and activities, and they are correct in this anticipation. Consequently, group members will press for that which is important to them, realizing other group members and their desires will

be a moderating influence. The fundamental principle in bargaining strategy is to ask for more than you expect to get and are willing to accept. Group members know this, and it is one reason that individuals in the group usually accept leader judgments that temporize their initial position. When a group member cannot accept the outcome, the member usually severs affiliation with the group.

5. A group setting is conducive to exaggeration. Exaggeration of benefits accruing to the group, threats to its existence or performance, and praise or criticism of the group will occur informally and travel rapidly in a group environment. This is due in part to what the group and its participants hear versus what is being said. There is a tendency to amplify the good news or bad news from member to member in cross discussions as each group member wants to be sure each other group member reacts with the same degree of understanding and intensity as everyone else does. Usually the loudest, not necessarily the most rational, voice dominates. You can attain a 'fever pitch' faster in a group setting than you can in dealing with individuals on a one-on-one basis.

6. A group setting is conducive to polarized thinking. Ideas, suggestions, or opinions presented to groups are usually accepted or rejected in totality, rather than analyzed for positive and negative elements. A large group is an excellent base for criticism but is less so for creative implementation, except for brainstorming sessions. Most group members will recognize extreme positions or ideas, but between the two 'poles' group members will differentiate and place themselves, making it difficult to find the exact solution acceptable to most members. Consequently, many decisions coming from a group represent the 'least detrimental' rather than the 'most far-reaching' position.

7. Contagion is rapidly and easily accomplished in a group setting. Groups are given to impulsive behavior more than the average individual. There is a greater impetus to transform suggestions into action and demand immediate achievement. This is due in part to the stimulation each participant enjoys from being a group member and the tendency toward emotionalism that stems from being in an interpersonal setting. Frequently, this desire for action manifests itself in the demand for appointment of subcommittees since most group members recognize the limitations of large groups.

8. A group will structure itself with respect to the roles participants play in group meetings. As group members become

familiar with one another through communication inter-change, they will establish their own niche in group activity. For example, one participant will frequently remind others of the basic objectives of the group in analyzing the current discussion or activity for focus on those objectives. Almost every group has, and needs, a person who provides comic relief. Someone will act informally as parliamentarian if a formal designation has not been made, and many participants will settle into their roles. Once developed, it's difficult for individual members to change their niche. If they attempt to change, initial efforts will be met with some degree of chastisement by other group members because change represents a disrupting impact on existing group dynamics.

9. Groups rely heavily on symbols. Recognizing that people are more transitory than institutions and desiring an allegiance to an impersonal representation of the group, rather than blind loyalty to a leader, symbolization plays a major role in congealing the group. The use of symbols can transcend differences among individuals within the group and act as a unifying element for the total group. Symbols represent visually the 'higher purpose' for which the group exists and can go a long way in preventing fractioning of the group. An organization's logo, flag, and statues are examples of such need-fulfilling symbols.

"I'll summarize this discussion of group behavior with

THE WIZARD'S WORDS OF MANAGEMENT WISDOM #42

Group effectiveness usually falls between the maximum possible and the minimum excusable. The result rests with the leadership in the wise use of group dynamics to achieve what is best achieved in a group setting. Sometimes it's better not to assemble a group. Other times, it's better to precondition individuals as to what you want accomplished prior to group assembly. "

"You are absolutely right, Winning Wizard," blurted Redael. "I have seen each of those dynamics occur several times in the various meetings I have attended. It's uncanny, but groups do behave that way."

Situations

"NOW THAT WE HAVE DISCUSSED several aspects of leaders and groups, Redael, we must turn our attention to the third, and equally elusive, element of the leadership syndrome—the situation. At the outset, we must state the obvious. Whereas leadership characteristics are bound by the personality, depth, and range of talent and flexibility of the person occupying the leadership position, and the group character tends to change only as the leadership changes or individual members enter and leave the setting, situations are highly volatile, fluid, and fleeting. In fact, the 'situation' is never static but is perpetually changing since it encompasses both the external and internal environments. Still, situations can be analyzed and categorized, and it behooves the leader to approach all 'situations' as being manageable.

"One must first consider factors over which the organization has virtually little or no control. Such factors include an abrupt change in the world or national economy, the issuance of a new governmental regulation, resource scarcity such as a utility cut down, the appearance of a competitor in the same market area, natural disasters, and so on. There are some external factors, however, over which the organization can exert some control. These include becoming involved in community activities; having employees run for local office; sponsoring local, regional, or national events that invite good public exposure; and things of that nature. This is known as being proactive.

"Internally, events can also occur over which the organization has little or no control. Examples are heavy employee absence due to illness such as the flu or destruction of company assets due to a calamity such as a flood or fire. Finally, the internal environment can change because of factors that are generated internally. Examples would be decisions to enter new market areas, expand the product or service line, change human resource policies, or acquire or divest divisions or subsidiaries. Given these four aspects of organizational existence, we can set up a matrix of possibilities as follows:

ENVIRONMENT

External	Internal
Stable	Stable
Stable	Unstable
Unstable	Stable
Unstable	Unstable

1. **Stable–Stable Environment.** This represents the most desired state—what most people refer to when they say 'it's business as usual.' External and internal elements are predictable, and a slight change on one side of the environment is balanced quickly and accurately by adaptation on the other side. Changes that do occur are planned or forecast, and there are no big waves in the organizational waters. A state of flux always exists, of course. That's why we have daily reports. Generally speaking, however, the systems used by an organization are working, and an atmosphere of relative calm and normalcy prevails. The leader enjoys the finest luxury—time. Harsh authoritarian and autocratic methods will meet with spoken or unspoken employee rejection. A solicitous or nonexcitable approach by management is expected and may even be appreciated.

2. **Stable–Unstable Environment.** This is the next easiest situation to manage since the focus can be on the internal instability with only normal attention being given externally until the in-house situation is remedied. Depending on the nature of the

internal instability, management can activate the contingency plan. Yes, that's right, you need contingency plans. Many matters of internal instability reside in the personnel area and can be overcome by promotion, transfer, reorganization, overtime, temporary hiring, use of consultants, or change of personnel policies. In such circumstances, the leader must, and is expected to, act quickly and decisively. You've got to preplan. Authoritative action carried out quickly and efficiently gives rise to the group's perception of your 'habit of command' and can reinforce your charisma.

3. **Unstable–Stable Environment.** This represents a frustrating management problem in that instability in the external environment is largely perceived as being beyond the influence and control of the leader–manager. The singular benefit is that the internal organizational environment is relatively stable, allowing for primary focus on the outside. It is under this situation that many leaders mentally, if not physically, capitulate to circumstances and operate under the 'I can't do anything about it' syndrome. The true leader rises to the occasion and guides the organizational ship through the stormy waters of unpredictability. This involves complete and efficient communication flow from subordinates as well as outside sources, so that assessment of the situation can be kept current. Decision making in an unpredictable environment is hazardous at best and catastrophic at worst. Sometimes the best decision under such conditions is to do nothing different until the situation clarifies. The world cannot stand incessant unpredictability, and consequently the external environment will 'settle down' after a relatively short time, although some irreversible changes may have taken place. The leader may need to 'buy time' as best one can because precipitous decisions can be as disastrous as procrastination. However, one cannot be immobilized, and consistent recognition of that point when it is necessary to act or not to act is what separates astute leaders from all the others.

4. **Unstable–Unstable Environment.** This represents the 'worst case' situation and often stems from the cause-and-effect relationship of the external environment on the organization. Bankruptcies and dissolutions do occur. This situation calls for leadership heroics and one whale of a lot of luck, but good leaders have a hand in making their own luck. Strong authoritarianism is essential, is expected, and is perceived as a resilient sinew. Management attention must be fairly equally

divided between the inside and outside environment, as changes in one area will necessitate a balancing action in the other. The greatest financial and human tolls are extracted in such circumstances but so are the greatest satisfactions. The external environment is likely to settle first. This situation often results in the mental and sometimes physical resignation of management. It is under such circumstances that your world sees what you're made of. The ultimate measure of management is at hand.

"Well, Redael, let's sum up this discussion of the situation with

THE WIZARD'S WORDS OF MANAGEMENT WISDOM #43

The effective leader affects the situation in far greater measure than the situation affects the leader."

"That's right, Winning Wizard!" Redael exclaimed. "I've seen that happen, too. Some people just seem to assume command, and others let them assume it.

"I'm really getting a lot out of this. Let's keep going," Redael urged.

Bureaucracy

"AS YOU KNOW, REDAEL, organizations are hierarchical structures, and workflows within such structures generally follow an input–throughput–output pattern. There is a concept that identifies this process, and it's called 'bureaucracy,'" Winning Wizard stated, jaws drawing tight. "Now that we have discussed the dynamics of leadership, groups, and the situation we need to turn our attention to an understanding of bureaucracy so you will be able to manage it to a productive end. Definitions first, Redael, so we have a basis for developing our insight," said Winning Wizard.

"A bureaucracy can be defined as 'an organized system of bureaus, divisions, or departments, each overviewing a prescribed functional area and scope of activity for which it has authority to act, coordination of which occurs through a stepped series of higher level responsibility and authority centers, the culmination of which is vested in the highest office.' That's a mouthful, I know, but that's the way it is.

"Bureaucracy has one striking feature. It exists in every realm of organized human activity. Before I proceed, it's necessary to state

THE WIZARD'S WORDS OF MANAGEMENT WISDOM #44

Bureaucracy is essential to the efficient and effective functioning of institutions. Its efficacy needs to be measured in terms of its concept as well as in terms of its conduct.

"Those words are self-evident if you stop to think about them. Bureaucracy is the natural outgrowth of the specialization of labor, which itself evolved as the result of the industrial and agrarian revolutions and the development of society. The advent of the concept of labor specialization was as significant to management science as the discovery of fire and the invention of the wheel were to physical science. As labor specialization proliferated, the need for unity of direction and coordination of effort became obvious. The tiered organization that we now speak of as a bureaucracy evolved as it met those needs. Bureaucracy has its advantages and disadvantages, like everything else. Here are some of its advantages:

1. Bureaucracy allows for a division of labor, which generates a high level of individual expertise.

2. Authority can be delegated, but responsibility cannot, and resources can be allocated to the different offices or bureaus.

3. Bureaucracy provides for review or appeal procedures and lower-level activity and decisions can be scrutinized by higher levels of authority. Ideas can be refined. Errors can be remedied.

4. Policies can be developed to address frequently arising issues.

5. Standards can be established to apply uniformity throughout the organization.

6. Economies of scale can benefit those the organization serves.

7. Monumental objectives can be reached through a directed, concerted unity of effort. A collective of linked individuals is stronger and is capable of an enlarged scope of activity relative to a series of isolated, unconnected individuals.

8. Responsibility and specific authority can be pinpointed and documented, and performance can be measured, individually and collectively.

"Here are some of the disadvantages, of which you must also be cognizant, Redael.

1. Labor specialization can reduce acceptance of personal responsibility by employees for the total end product or service.

2. Employee perceptions of the stated objectives can be widely diverse.

3. Policy application and the meeting of regulations can become ends in themselves rather than the means to the end of serving those the organization purports to serve.

4. Communication and coordination are susceptible to distortion in multi-tiered 'vertical structures.'

5. Personal service can give way to impersonal 'red tape' processing.

6. Bureaucrats sell their services to the organization in return for a paycheck and may have no stake, or pride in ownership, which can result in labor turnover. This can be assuaged in the private sector, however, by stock options, profit sharing, and pension plans.

7. The decision-making process is often slow and cumbersome.

8. 'Staff' specialists may not really understand 'line' or operational problems on which they are asked to assist, and operations personnel may not understand staff specialties and language.

"The design of bureaucracy is not nearly as important as the ability of the leader to measure its performance against predetermined objectives.

"Well, Redael, here are

THE WIZARD'S WORDS OF MANAGEMENT WISDOM #45

The smaller the organization, the greater the personal duty placed on the leader. The larger the organization, the greater the management responsibility placed on the leader."

"I've always regarded the word 'bureaucracy' as pejorative, Winning Wizard," Redael volunteered. "But it does have its good points, too. Interesting!"

Leaders Versus Bureaucrats

"REDAEL, NOW THAT WE HAVE TALKED about leadership, groups, situations, and bureaucracies, I feel compelled to point out some differences between leaders and bureaucrats," Winning Wizard opined with a slight touch of disdain. "It's all in the mindset and the approach to life and work.

"Allow me to point out some contrasts between leaders and bureaucrats to illustrate the differences.

1. Leaders say, 'We can do it.' Bureaucrats say, 'It'll never work!'

2. Leaders look for continued progress. Bureaucrats are overly proud of the status quo.

3. Leaders exhibit and inspire an improvement attitude. Bureaucrats are self-satisfied.

4. Leaders look for opportunities. Bureaucrats wait for something to happen.

5. Leaders 'play a good game.' Bureaucrats 'talk a good game.'

6. Leaders judge themselves. Bureaucrats hope others will judge them favorably.

7. Leaders know they must confront problems. Bureaucrats hope problems will go away.

8. Leaders demand flawless administration. Bureaucrats get bogged down in administrivia.

9. Leaders delegate duties and tasks. Bureaucrats absorb duties and tasks.

10. Leaders are comfortable with their subordinates. Bureaucrats are comfortable in their offices.

11. A leader says, 'I'm responsible.' A bureaucrat says, 'It's not my fault.'

12. Leaders can laugh at themselves. Bureaucrats are offended by bureaucracy-directed humor.

13. A leader shares credit. A bureaucrat claims the credit.

14. A leader says, 'I'll take the blame.' The bureaucrat says, 'Who's to blame?'

15. The leader is a tireless worker. The bureaucrat is a tired worker.

16. When things get hot, the leader is overwhelming. When things get hot, the bureaucrat is overwhelmed.

17. The leader goes for 'the win.' The bureaucrat goes for 'the tie.'

18. The leader rises above adversity. The bureaucrat runs away from adversity.

19. The leader is outgoing. The bureaucrat likes going out.

20. The leader is often the team's 'most valuable player.' The bureaucrat is often the team's 'most voluble player.'

21. Leaders develop subordinates. Bureaucrats assign subordinates.

22. Leaders say, 'We can fix that.' Bureaucrats say, 'I told you it wouldn't work.'

23. Leaders are customer oriented. Bureaucrats are process oriented.

24. Leaders provide direction. Bureaucrats give instructions.

25. Leaders can manage many things at once. Bureaucrats prefer to manage one thing at a time.

26. Leaders can handle the media effectively. Bureaucrats allow the media to handle them.

27. Leaders earn respect. Bureaucrats demand respect.

28. Leaders seek organizational commitment and loyalty. Bureaucrats require personal commitment and loyalty.

29. Leaders trust key subordinates. Bureaucrats rely on control systems.

30. Leaders plan for the future. Bureaucrats let the future unfold.

31. Leaders recruit the best talent available. Bureaucrats don't want to be challenged by subordinates.

32. Leaders teach. Bureaucrats pontificate.

33. Leaders emphasize standards. Bureaucrats emphasize discipline.

34. Leaders focus. Bureaucrats watch.

35. Leaders inspire. Bureaucrats perspire.

36. Leaders manage the stress in their lives. Bureaucrats are managed by the stress in their lives.

37. Leaders communicate articulately. Bureaucrats communicate artfully.

38. Leaders lead for the future. Bureaucrats manage for the moment.

39. Leaders take action at the appropriate time. Bureaucrats react only when necessary.

40. Leaders say, 'We succeeded in spite of the obstacles.' Bureaucrats say, 'We could have succeeded, if it hadn't been for the obstacles.'

41. Leaders take advantage of the rules. Bureaucrats go strictly by the rules.

42. Leaders see the glass as half full. Bureaucrats don't see the glass.

43. Leaders are generous with their time. Bureaucrats are protective of their time.

44. When things look as if they are going wrong, leaders cry, 'charge!' When things look as if they are going wrong, bureaucrats cry, 'foul!'

45. Leaders are gracious. Bureaucrats are ingratiating.

46. Leaders are aggressive. Bureaucrats are intrusive.

47. Leaders think strategically. Bureaucrats think about time off.

48. Leaders attempt to be objective. Bureaucrats can be swayed and influenced.

49. Leaders are selflessly motivated. Bureaucrats are selfishly motivated.

50. Leaders enjoy their time. Bureaucrats put in their time.

"All in all, Redael, one of the very best pieces of advice I can ever give you can be found in

The Wizard's Words of Management Wisdom #46

Don't ever allow your organization to be run by bureaucrats."

"That's astounding, Winning Wizard," said a nearly overwhelmed Redael. "You are right on point. I run into a lot of bureaucrats, and you've described them perfectly. I'm never going to let that happen in my organization."

The Door

"LET'S TALK ABOUT an employee relations technique, Redael, that I have found to be a myth and therefore organizationally detrimental," noted Winning Wizard, shaking his head and gritting his teeth.

"I have known a number of managers who, because they read it or heard it somewhere and thought it sounded nice, professed to have an 'open door' policy in their organization as part of the relationship they attempted to foster with their employees. In one specific case, I was told by one of my managers, 'I have an open door policy in this organization. My people can get to me at any time about anything!'

"On the face of it, this exclamation seems virtuous, democratic, pleasant to say, and pleasant to hear. The only trouble is that this 'policy' **doesn't work,** and I have never known anyone who professed it to really live by it. In fact, I have known managers who became the object of derision by employees as the result of their management hypocrisy based on the divergence of stated philosophy with actual performance.

"Let's analyze this 'policy,' Redael, in light of its intent, content, and desirability. Clearly, it behooves you to create an environment in which all your employees feel they can, and in fact can, see you concerning matters for which they have not gained satisfaction and for which you could assist. The additional psychological advantage is obvious, of course, in that the employee's perception of self-importance and organizational concern are heightened since you have made your time available. If an employee visits you in your office, the physical trappings are often enough to cause the employee to minimize the problem and to absorb every word you utter as though it's the gospel. No matter what the outcome, the fact that you listened and perhaps extolled is organizationally supportive and reinforcing in and of itself. Those are the advantages.

"However, if you allowed this procedure to operate unchecked and without control, you could get little else accomplished and you'd have to replace your carpet or tile all too frequently. Still, to have an 'open door' policy and then keep the door closed is self-defeating. You may counter, Redael, by saying that many problems can be solved directly at lower operating levels or with staff assistance and should not be brought to your attention in the first place. True enough! Unfortunately, however, many employees will not accept a decision as final until it reaches the pinnacle of the organization.

"It's not really a dilemma, Redael, if you remember

The Wizard's Words of Management Wisdom #47

Do not have an 'open door' policy; rather, have an 'accessible door' policy. Make it clear that you are not available at any time for any thing but that you can be made available if absolutely necessary, only after all other possible remedies and resources have been applied. You are no more 'interruptible' than is the employee in the course of his or her normal duty performance.

"While I'm thinking about it, Redael, permit me to make another point about employee relations," exclaimed the sage. "It's

THE WIZARD'S WORDS OF MANAGEMENT WISDOM #48

Every manager should meet personally every new employee assigned to that manager's physical location on the date of hire or as close thereto as possible. Area, district, or regional managers should meet personally at each location new employees who have been hired since the date of the last visit. It's a wise investment in human capital."

"Good points, Winning Wizard," stated Redael, jotting down notes. "My door will be an accessible door, and I'll make it a tenet of mine to meet new employees whenever and wherever I can."

Controlling Controls

"THE WORD 'CONTROL' REDAEL, has a variety of meanings, yet most people think of it, initially anyway, in its negative sense. In organizations, control is usually equated with a restraint or restriction on what one is allowed to do. The regulatory sense of the word has a bad connotation, as in the phrase 'they control everyone who works for them.' We take that to mean that there was a manipulative or disproportionate influence or restraint to the working relationship that would place the subordinate in the role of a mechanical instrument or a puppet. Most of the meanings of 'control' are, in fact, not negative. For example, in scientific research, a **control group,** as opposed to an experimental group, is the basis of measurement against which the results of the experiment can be determined. The **controls** of a vehicle govern its direction, speed, turning capability, and so on. In the management sense, 'control' means a system of orderliness and organizational discipline and functioning in combination with internal and external security measures. It is not repressive or restrictive; rather, it is illuminating as it assigns responsibility and, therefore, highlights proper functioning as well as malfunctioning. We will now discuss controls with a three-part

THE WIZARD'S WORDS OF MANAGEMENT WISDOM #49

1. Control is necessary for good employee morale.

2. Any control system can be beaten.

3. The control system should not cost more than the value of the loss it's designed to prevent.

1. **Control is necessary for good employee morale.** Since a good control system offers checks and balances within the organization, it encourages and supports honesty. At some time in your life, Redael, I am sure you have been a member of a group in which it was discovered that something within the organization, be it a club, barracks, dormitory, office, plant, etc., turned up missing—presumably stolen! You knew that you didn't do it, but no one else, except the thief, knew that you didn't do it, and you, along with all the other group members, were suspect. Why? Because there was no control system that definitely assigned responsibility. You know what a demoralizing and frustrating feeling it is to have the cloud of suspicion hanging over your head with no way to prove your innocence.

2. **Any control system can be beaten.** Mechanical and electronic controls can be interrupted, paper controls can be doctored, or records can be duplicated. Computer controls can be bypassed or broken into, and visual control can be rendered impotent by collusion or payoff. There is a story about the department manager of a large organization who insisted that no subordinates could leave their desks at the end of the day unless the desktops were completely clear of the day's work. Not only that, but the manager would periodically inspect desk drawers just before closing to be sure that subordinates were not sitting on projects and simply stuffing work in the drawers in order to have a clean desktop. How's that for a control system, Redael? It was beaten easily. The subordinates simply placed all of their work in the mail envelope for the intrafirm mail system 15 minutes before quitting time, addressed the envelope to themselves, and mailed it, thereby leaving their desktops clean and their drawers relatively empty. They would receive their own work back through the house mail at 8:30 the next morning. You see the point.

3. **The control system should not cost more than the value of the loss it's designed to prevent.** The 'cost' is not only a dollar cost. It also applies to time, space, and employee utilization. It makes no sense to design an elaborate and expensive control system to preclude the loss of a minuscule amount of money or merchandise. A manager once reprimanded an employee, 'I think you are ignoring our control system,' to which the employee replied, 'Yes, but somebody has to get the work done.' You can't afford to build an overhead to monitor a control system that is more cumbersome than the activity it monitors."

"A lot of this is common sense, Winning Wizard," Redael stated, with a measure of confidence. "I think everyone knows about these things."

"Actually, Redael, in organizational life, common sense is not always that common," Winning Wizard remarked. "Just think for a moment, my friend, about all the bright people we have in our organizations, who supposedly have common sense, but we still get into so many dumb situations," Winning Wizard lamented.

"I see, Winning Wizard, I see your point," said Redael, confirming another insight.

"It also appears that over-control can inhibit personal and systemic productivity," Redael said. "How do I ensure high productivity in the organization, Winning Wizard?"

Producing Productivity Productively

"SINCE YOU ASKED, REDAEL, I'll give you my thoughts on the subject of 'productivity,'" said Winning Wizard, eyes sparkling. "It's a topic of increasing interest and concern, and I'll approach it using a metaphor. Definitions first, so we both start from the same base. It's been stated frequently that there are three ways to increase productivity:

1. Maintain the same level of output with a reduced level of input.

2. Increase the level of output while maintaining the same level of input.

3. Increase the level of input slightly to yield a disproportionately larger level of output. This is often referred to as part of the 'economies of scale' concept and/or 'leveraging.'

"There is a fourth possibility, theoretically, but it's not always practical for business use. That would be to rapidly decrease input with a slower decrease in output so the 'productivity margin' widens in the short run. This is usually self-defeating, however, unless it is part of a phase-out or longer-term exit strategy.

"So much for definitions. Also note, Redael, that inputs and outputs can be expressed in a number of ways, such as dollars made or saved, hours worked, customers served, products made, number of employees, sales per employee, and so forth.

"Let's take a hypothetical case and apply a combination of these ideas. We'll use baseball as the example. That's right, Redael, you heard me correctly. Baseball!

"Baseball needs to be more productive. Solution number 1: Have a pitcher and a catcher and no other fielders. You've just saved seven salaries. That's reduced input. The batters who come up to the plate would all be .300 hitters, if not .800 or .900 hitters, which would be good for the gate and baseball's statistics. That's increased output. Further productivity gains could be achieved by eliminating the catcher, since a resilient backstop could return the ball.

"Don't like that solution, Redael? OK, here's another alternative. Solution number 2: Keep 9 people on the team, which maintains the same input, but expand the normal game to 12 innings and allow each team 6 outs in their half of the inning. That way there would be more turns at bat, more pitches, more fielding chances, and more 'big' plays, which results in increased output.

"Don't like that one either, Redael? All right, let me try solution number 3: Put 10 people on a team and have 4 outs per half inning. That's slightly increased input. You can expect many more runs, many more strikeouts, and many more customers, such as relatives and friends of the players. That results in greatly increased output.

"Then there is always that fourth but usually impractical solution number 4: Pack the ball park and then cancel the game without refunding the tickets, or give rain checks that are good only on rainy days. That could save players' and groundskeepers' salaries, which will drastically reduce input. This would widen your 'productivity margin'—remember, you didn't refund the money, and parking and food concessions would still operate, which is a slower decrease in output. Realize, of course, this action wouldn't result in pure profit, since you'd have increased expenses for fan riot control, stadium repair, and press relations.

"No, Redael, I don't have my foot in my mouth, but I do have my tongue in my cheek. You can see the patent absurdity to the foregoing silly proposals.

"I thought I would use a little humor to emphasize

THE WIZARD'S WORDS OF MANAGEMENT WISDOM #50

Productivity is not only a numbers concept. It's also a value concept, a point that is too often overlooked. Quality, not quantity, must be the dominant feature in contemplating productivity increases and methods to achieve them. The most productive organizations are the ones that are the most value conscious."

"That analogy does underscore your point, Winning Wizard," said Redael, chuckling. "Numbers are only numbers. I really need to look at the value effect behind them."

S.E.R.V.I.C.E.

"I WANT TO TALK TO YOU ABOUT the concept of S.E.R.V.I.C.E., Redael, which some people in our society and in this organization feel is declining," said Winning Wizard, almost dejectedly.

"Service is receiving increased attention these days as organizations attempt to gain or maintain a competitive edge in the marketplace. Survey after survey indicates the general public is critical of the services they receive, or perhaps do not receive, from retailers, public agencies, and other institutions with which they come into contact. At the same time, customers indicate they want better service and frequent those organizations where they believe they are getting a 'service value' as well as a 'product value' for their money. Since service is being touted as a point of competitive differentiation it behooves us to take a look at it, Redael, both in terms of its definition and its composition.

"Everyone has a definition of 'service' based on individual experiences. Service is often in the eyes and ears of the beholder. It may be hard to describe, but we know it when we experience it. Nevertheless, in order to establish a common base, I offer the following definition. 'Service' is correctly anticipating the needs and/or desires of customers and prospects, taking timely, appropriate action to fulfill or exceed those expectations to the complete satisfaction of the customer, resulting in the highest transaction exchange value possible and a positive predisposition for a continuing service relationship in the future.

"I know that sounds terribly academic, Redael, but it is comprehensive, as it needs to be.

"Now, let's turn our attention to the elements of service. There are seven of them, embodied in the word itself.

1. **Spirit** is what is required in the people who will be performing the service. It all starts with spirit. You need to recruit positively spirited people to your organization, train them, retain them, and constantly nurture the service culture and service attitude that should abound throughout the entire system.

2. **Empathy** is the ability of a service performer to place himself or herself in the mindset of the customer so that the server can sense, through observation, telepathy, or both, the needs and/or desires of the customer. It's that 'sixth sense' that needs to be operative because anticipation is a necessary step in the service process.

3. **Responsiveness** is taking timely and appropriate action to meet the expectations of the customers. Timeliness does not always means quickness, because sometimes proper pacing is more important than speed. Appropriate action requires a balance so that actions are not under-accomplished, nor are they overdone. A service performer should not 'short serve' a customer, be overbearing, or be excessively solicitous. Judgment is key.

4. **Visibility** of service is required because the customer needs to feel that he or she is being served and that everyone in the entire environment knows that service acts are occurring. That's what gives an organization a pleasant 'hum' of activity that makes people, both customers and service performers, glad they are a part of it.

5. **Inventiveness** is sometimes required to perform good service. It may be doing a little something extra, such as overriding a system to resolve an unusual problem or following up on something at a later time. Your service performers need to be invention-minded since everything they encounter will not fit into predesigned service programs, packages, and policies.

6. **Competency** is essential for good service to be sustained and to thrive. The customer assumes competency on the part of the service performer, and if it is not evident, a disservice occurs, which exacerbates a worsening situation. Service performers need to possess and exude gracious competency to initiate the server–customer relationship on a basis of mutual respect.

7. **Enthusiasm** is the crowning touch service performers need to maximize the transaction exchange value with the customer during the immediate interface. Soaring enthusiasm is good for everyone—the organization, the customer, and the server. It ties back closely to **Spirit,** which completes the service loop, and causes customers to reflect well on their experience and want to come back.

"That's it, Redael," noted Winning Wizard matter-of-factly. "Easy in concept, more difficult in execution.

"Always try to remember

THE WIZARD'S WORDS OF MANAGEMENT WISDOM #51

S.E.R.V.I.C.E. equals P.R.O.F.I.T.S. —people returning often for insured total satisfaction. "

"Remember it, I will, Winning Wizard," said Redael excitedly.

"That's a great way to look at 'service' and 'profits.' I am really learning a lot, Winning Wizard. Let's keep going."

Defining Moments

"THERE WILL BE A FEW INSTANCES in your professional life, Redael, that will make an indelible mark on you and the way you progress through your career," said Winning Wizard. "They are defining moments because the way in which you respond identifies your core being as a person, and the world will know what you are made of.

"I want to give you some issues that you are likely to face, not because I expect an answer from you now, but because I want to provoke your thinking so you can be ready for them when they occur," said the teacher to the pupil.

"OK, Winning Wizard. I'm ready. Go ahead," said Redael, feeling slightly challenged.

"Here they are, my young friend," said Winning Wizard, eyes peering over lowered reading glasses.

1. An employee has not been performing well, and a termination is in order. Do you tell the employee that the cause of termination is a general reorganization or an overall reduction of personnel, or do you actually state to the employee the elements of the malperformance that have led to this dismissal?

2. Your purchasing manager has dealt with Company A for a considerable period of time and has received good quality and good service. It's been a good relationship. A salesperson for Company B visits and can match Company A's quality, service, and price schedule. The Company B salesperson also indicates Company B is holding a week-long seminar in 2 months for its major customers (spouses included) at a luxurious resort. Your purchasing manager would be invited 'once the order is placed.' You become aware of the situation. Do you do anything? If so, what?

3. A job applicant from another city visits you for an interview. By happenstance, you learn that the applicant is also interviewing with other organizations in your area on this trip. The applicant sends you the full cost of the trip with copies of the airfare stub, hotel bill, meals, and airport parking. What do you do?

4. A Human Resources department employee in charge of the company suggestion system receives an excellent suggestion that will benefit the company. The HR employee tells a friend, another employee, about the suggestion and further tells that second employee how to change the suggestion just enough so it doesn't 'look copied' and to backdate it, so the second employee will receive the cash award and recognition. You become aware of what's happened. How do you address it?

5. A loyal, long-standing organizational subordinate brings you an insignificant gift, say a small desk ornament. You think nothing of it. Then it happens again a short while later, but it's a little larger gift this time and it's personal. How do you handle it?

6. You are traveling with a co-worker for the first time. The co-worker seems to be a solid type. You complete your assignment in the far away city late in the day. You will fly back tomorrow. You go out to dinner with the co-worker who then becomes an entirely different person and begins to do some things totally out of character and that are alien to your interest, values, and lifestyle. What do you do?

7. A co-worker in charge of production begins shaving 2% off the weight of a product and leaves out a minor and relatively insignificant ingredient that does not affect the safety of the product. These 'shavings' are imperceptible to customers, and there are no extraordinary complaints. Still, it's not up

to established standards. The co-worker justifies such action as necessary to 'make cost.' How do you address this? Or do you address it? If so, to whom do you address it?

8. A large and important customer contacts you soliciting a contribution for an organization in which, although worthy, you have no particular interest or affiliation. The customer suggests an amount that is well beyond the scale of your capability. What do you say, and how and in what environment do you say it?

9. This a three-part question.
   A. A large, long-standing, and important supplier calls you and indicates that a close relative is looking for work. You have never met the relative nor do you know anything about the person. The supplier states, 'I would consider it a personal favor and would be mighty proud if my relative could be a part of your company.' You do have some positions open. How do you handle this?
   B. Later that same day, you get a call from a politician, say, the mayor of the city, who extols on the virtues of your suppliers' relative. Thus, you become aware of the 'political' connection. What do you say to the politician?
   C. Assuming you meet with the supplier's relative, you will come to a decision. You will either hire the person or you won't. Assume you don't. What do you say to the applicant? Do you also communicate to the supplier? If so, how do you handle it? Do you also communicate with the politician?

10. In a large meeting at which you are in attendance, the person presiding over the meeting starts by enthusiastically speaking about a major accomplishment that has occurred in which you unquestionably played the major lead role. In the comments, the person presiding mentions the name of one of your colleagues who was involved but only in a very minor way. The person presiding continues, incorrectly, to lavish praise on this person, and inexplicably, your colleague begins to bask in the glow and says nothing. What do you do, if anything, and when and how do you do it?

11. At an organizational social occasion at which males and females are present and at which some important outsiders are also in attendance, one of the attendees captures attention and proceeds to tell a decidedly off-color and graphic joke that contains foul language. What do you do if:
   A. The person is part of your organization?
   B. The person is one of the outside guests?

12. A long-term employee of average capability and performance suddenly hits the wall of non-productivity. The problem does not appear to be health related, mental, or physical, and, as far as you know, there is nothing amiss in the employee's personal life. You ask for the employee's personnel file folder. Surprisingly, you find that the employee just turned 64 years old. The employee doesn't look it at all. Normal retirement age is 65. What do you do?

13. You go out to bid on one of your contracts or agreements every 3 years. The bidding process will soon begin. On your birthday, you receive a stunningly beautiful gift from the incumbent contractor, well beyond what even your own family members would give you. You don't know exactly, but you have a fair idea of the price range. Expensive! What do you do?

14. It has come to your attention that one of your organizational associates is engaged in 'backbiting' and you are the target. It starts with half-truths and progresses to accusations of incompetency: 'he/she's not really that good, all front and no substance.' What do you do if the backbiter is:
A. A higher level manager, but not your boss?
B. On the same organizational level as you are in your department?
C. Is a subordinate but in another department?
D. On the same organizational level as you are but in another department?

15. An inspector enters your premises; takes several notes; and cites multiple 'violations' that are marginal at worst, are highly debatable, and/or can be rectified on the spot. The inspector states, 'This is really a shame. I hate to have to do this. It's too bad there's not a way we can work it out. I'd like to be able to work it out in some way.' The inspector looks at you expectantly for your response. How do you handle it?

16. A position becomes available to which you have long aspired. You are 'hands down' the most qualified person to take the position, and most observers have the expectation it will fall to you. Inexplicably the offer is extended to another person, who accepts. What do you do? Resign? Castigate or undermine the other person? Deride the process? Deny your interest? Silently grit your teeth and continue doing what you are doing? Vow to have revenge? Become an ardent supporter of the new person? Cease communication? Champion the organization all the more?

17. A steady and reliable customer pays down the current balance of your receivable. Two weeks later a second check arrives in the same amount. There has been a duplicate payment. What do you do with the check? Return it? Deposit it? Write out your check and send it with a letter of explanation as to what it represents—that is, a refund of a duplicate payment? How quickly do you take the action you're going to take?

18. An organizational colleague, with whom you have strained relations because that person embarrassed you or did not treat you well in the past, is in a serious predicament. You are in a position to measurably help that person. You know that, and the person also knows that. There has not been a request for your assistance. What do you do? Let the person hang? Do nothing, unless there is a request for your help? Refuse assistance? Volunteer support? Assist without anyone knowing it?

19. In the process of recruiting a senior-level executive to join your organization, you are a member of a committee that meets, greets, and dines with the recruit. Over a meal, in his zeal to woo the person to the organization, a colleague expounds about an aspect of the organization that you know is not true. What do you do?

20. A subordinate comes to you and somewhat sheepishly indicates that one of her peers, a male, is making conversation and comments that make her feel uncomfortable. The comments are nothing blatant, direct, or overt, just certain phrases, not even 'purple prose.' She is reluctant to say she is being harassed. The word she keeps using is 'uncomfortable.' What is your next step?

21. You are part of a two-person project team. Your partner pleads a busy schedule, so you wind up doing most of the work. The finished work product is in the hands of your team member and the panel to whom it is to be presented. At the presentation, your colleague seizes the moment and dominates the presentation. Your colleague has mastered your work well and presents it accurately. At the conclusion, you both receive appropriate, equal credit and 'well dones.' Do you say anything to anyone? To whom? When?

"Well, I think you see the point, Redael," concluded Winning Wizard, with a touch of voice fatigue. "You will face these types of things with some frequency."

"I must confess, Winning Wizard, that I'm a little shaken listening to these examples. I really am going to have to think them through very carefully," said a crestfallen Redael.

"That's my purpose, Redael, to have you prethink vexing situations and not go into them blindly," Winning Wizard exclaimed. "It may help if you always remember these two

THE WIZARD'S WORDS OF MANAGEMENT WISDOM # 52

You can never defend a wrong, but often what is right needs a lot of defense.

THE WIZARD'S WORDS OF MANAGEMENT WISDOM # 53

Make any defining moment you encounter a fine moment."

Bosses

"AS YOU PROGRESS IN YOUR CAREER, Redael, you will be exposed to a number of bosses," cautioned Winning Wizard to the young protégé. "I think you would be wise to think of them in the same light as they think of themselves. I have assembled 100 'virtues' of being a boss, which you may find interesting and perhaps a bit humorous. Here they are:

1. Bosses are never insensitive—they are just being objective.

2. Bosses are never egotistical—they just possess stratospheric self-esteem.

3. Bosses are never indecisive—they just weigh all the alternatives very, very carefully.

4. Bosses are never reckless—they're courageous.

5. Bosses never take a break—they just want to experience a change of pace.

6. Bosses never take a vacation—they do external market research.

7. Bosses never get angry—they become concerned.

8. Bosses are never volatile—they just have a broad range of emotions.

9. Bosses are never nit picky—they are detail conscious.

10. Bosses are never wrong—they are given faulty or incomplete information.

11. Bosses are never late—they were just taking care of a little problem.

12. Bosses never relax—they are just contemplating the future from a different vantage point.

13. Bosses are never impatient—they just excel at time management.

14. Bosses are never critical—they are constructively helpful.

15. Bosses are never speechless—they are just weighing their words carefully.

16. Bosses never experience self-doubt—they are just reassessing the situation.

17. Bosses are never radical—they're creative.

18. Bosses are never flashy—they're stylish.

19. Bosses are never confused—they are just sorting out the facts.

20. Bosses are never rash—they're action oriented.

21. Bosses are never stingy—they're prudent.

22. Bosses never get nervous—they just have a high intensity level.

23. Bosses are never without an answer—they just approach matters by asking questions.

24. Bosses never register surprise—they register calculated spontaneity.

25. Bosses never leave early—they are on their way to a meeting.

26. Bosses are never frustrated—they are determined.

27. Bosses are never arrogant—they are self-confident.

28. Bosses are never whimsical—they have vision.

29. Bosses are never pessimistic—they are realistic.

30. Bosses are never unrealistic—they're optimistic.

31. Bosses are never skeptical—they're practical.

32. Bosses are never forgetful—they were just going to address the matter at a later time.

33. Bosses never lose self-control—they're just being dynamic.

34. Bosses never fail to be understanding—they understand only too well.

35. Bosses are never inconsistent—they're flexible.

36. Bosses never interrogate—they're just curious.

37. Bosses are never reclusive—they're just in a planning session.

38. Bosses never negotiate—they dictate.

39. Bosses don't get sick—they rest.

40. Bosses never preach—they teach.

41. Bosses never demand—they suggest.

42. Bosses never get in the way—they just want to be kept involved.

43. Bosses are never driven—they're motivated.

44. Bosses are never fierce—they're tenacious.

45. Bosses never work harder—they work smarter.

46. Bosses never become distracted—they're just generating different ideas.

47. Bosses never sleep—they meditate.

48. Bosses are never fixated—they're focused.

49. Bosses are never grouchy—they're resolute.

50. Bosses are never happy—they're temporarily satisfied.

51. Bosses are never slick—they're smooth.

52. Bosses don't just see things—they see through things.

53. Bosses don't just speak—they speak eloquently.

54. Bosses don't just hear what you are saying—they hear what you are not saying.

55. Bosses don't just feel—they absorb.

56. Bosses never pick up the check—they pick out the place.

57. Bosses never relegate—they delegate.

58. Bosses don't engage in gamesmanship—they engage in statesmanship.

59. Bosses don't just write—they exude.

60. Bosses never exaggerate—they just show things in the best possible light.

61. Bosses don't study—they are quick studies.

62. Bosses are never inattentive—they're preoccupied.

63. Bosses don't have idiosyncrasies—they have a management style.

64. Bosses are not rigid—they're consistent.

65. Bosses never retreat—they are just circling around another way.

66. Bosses are never speechless—they just realize that there is a time to speak and a time not to speak.

67. Bosses don't just stand behind subordinates—they also stand out front leading them.

68. Bosses don't just speedread—they speedthink.

69. Bosses don't just ingest information—they devour it.

70. Bosses never make errors—they have learning experiences.

71. Bosses never let someone or something get out of hand—they are just allowing a little more leash.

72. Bosses don't just do things right—they do the right things.

73. Bosses are never oblivious—they just choose to overlook it.

74. Bosses never hold a grudge—they just have long memories.

75. Bosses know when opportunity knocks—they don't knock the opportunities.

76. Bosses never overtalk their points—they're just completely thorough.

77. Bosses never undertalk their points—they just believe in brevity and letting the situation speak for itself.

78. Bosses never interrupt—they just want an immediate status report.

79. Bosses never get into a reactive mode—they are always in an active mode.

80. Bosses are never perplexed—they are just pausing until the right moment occurs.

81. Bosses never carry much money—but their associates do.

82. Bosses don't just think—they think big.

83. Bosses never wish—they make it happen.

84. Bosses never get ulcers—they give them.

85. Bosses never ask for help—they ask for teamwork and teamthink.

86. Bosses are never disorganized—they are just creative with work flows and communication patterns.

87. Bosses never have tight jaws, grit their teeth, or count to 10—they are just being strong in their restraint.

88. Bosses never make the same mistake twice—they are just reconfirming that history can repeat itself.

89. Bosses don't miscommunicate—others misunderstand.

90. Bosses are never stubborn—they just abide by unshakable principles.

91. Bosses are never sullen—they just have a lot on their minds.

92. Bosses are never nostalgic—they just keep referring to the past as a teaching tool for others.

93. Bosses never manipulate subordinates—they challenge them.

94. Bosses are never bossy—they are crisply direct.

95. Bosses never beat around the bush—they tell it like it is.

96. Nothing ever goes over the head of the boss or else it comes out from under the feet of subordinates.

97. Bosses are never bored—they just need to take a deep breath now and then.

98. Bosses are never funny—they just have a different sense of humor.

99. Bosses don't set constraints—they just want things to go through channels.

100. Bosses never pass the buck—they just want more research done.

"That's quite a list, Winning Wizard," said Redael, scurrying to get the last few words on paper. "I see what you're getting at. Depending on the level of your perch, you see things from different points of view."

"You're catching on quite quickly, Redael. I can see that you are a quick study," commented Winning Wizard. "I'll wrap this discussion up with

THE WIZARD'S WORDS OF MANAGEMENT WISDOM #54

Bosses are never exactly alike. Neither are they totally different."

The 12 Es

"READEL MY FRIEND, there are likely to be a number of 'first days' in your organizational life where you will assemble your full staff or department heads to meet for the first time in your role as their manager," Winning Wizard projected. "That first meeting is critical because it will set your subordinates' impressions and perceptions of you. You need to set the conditions, pace, standards, and ethics that you will demand of yourself and, by extension, what you expect of them. Here are some thoughts you may want to consider as you develop your remarks. I call them the 12 Es.

1. **Enthusiasm**—We need to exude enthusiasm both in our persona and for our mission and objectives of our organization, our function, and our tasks. Our enthusiasm can be contagious. If we are not enthusiastic, ennui can take hold in our organization and that can lead to mediocrity—or even decline.

2. **Energy**—Energy, I believe, is closely aligned with enthusiasm because it connotes movement, action, passion, and spirit. I have found that self-starters are usually strong finishers. Energy is the personal electric current we infuse into the workplace and marketplace.

3. **Excellence**—We will establish or exceed current standards of performance for ourselves in pursuit of overall organizational excellence. We will be politely but directly demanding of continuing professional and organizational improvement in search of perfection.

4. **Example**—We recognize that we are role models for our colleagues at all levels of the organization. Others look to us wanting to give us one of their most cherished possessions—their trust. We will never besmirch our credibility, for if we did, we would lose the trust of subordinates and our customers, and once trust is gone, there really is nothing left.

5. **Empathy**—We will place humanitarianism well ahead of materialism, people before artifacts, values before judgments, thoughts before action, and reason before decisions. Accordingly, we have or will develop the ability to step outside our own minds and into the minds of others, thereby seeing and understanding their perspectives, feeling their emotions, and relating to their activities.

6. **Effectiveness**—We know that what we do makes a difference. We will set or help to set a direction toward an attainable and sustainable goal, and we will get results. Our work service and work product reflect our knowledge, our skills, our talents, and our creativity, all devoted toward noticeable and measurable accomplishment.

7. **Efficiency**—We will maximize the most important commodity in our lives—time. We will also optimize our output, starting with the input and carefully managing the throughput. We will minimize waste, synergize resources, and symbolize dynamism.

8. **Empowerment**—Because we each possess expertise at what we do, there is a certain power that attaches to our roles and to our personas. We have the ability to empower others to do things, by delegation, by inspiration, or by direction. We will not abuse power. We will use it to serve others in fulfilling our organizational missions.

9. **Essentiality**—In our relationships with people we will apprise them by both word and action that we regard them as absolutely essential to the success of our organization. We will be highly oriented to our customers, both external and internal, and we will apprise our subordinates, irrespective of their

positions, titles, and levels within the organizational hierarchy, that they are an integral part of the success of our organization. If they were not essential, they wouldn't be with us.

10. **Esteem**—We possess or will develop self-esteem, and we will draw the esteem of others. As you know, esteem rests on the four cornerstones of integrity, character, self-confidence, and self-respect. We will place our greatest satisfaction in self-measurement, conduct ourselves with poise and dignity, have a high quality of life competence, and continue to develop our specific expertise.

11. **Equilibrium**—With all the stimuli that are directed to us, and all the stimuli we issue, we will maintain a stable balance in our intellectual, personal, professional, and physical life. We have self-control, and we are in shape, unflappable, fair, rational, caring, alert, forward thinking, responsible, and determined.

12. **Education**—We value education and training, recognizing that development for us and our subordinates is a journey, not a destination; a lifelong process, not a one-time event; dynamic, not static. If anyone ever doubts the value of continuing education and training, then consider the cost of ignorance.

"I urge you, Redael," implored the sage, "to always follow

THE WIZARD'S WORDS OF MANAGEMENT WISDOM #55

Eternally embrace every element of the 12 Es. "

"I will, Winning Wizard, I will," promised Redael, resolving to do so hereafter.

Euphemistically Yours

"I HAVE FOUND, REDAEL, that when people write something about someone else, they are extremely careful and guarded in what they put on paper," Winning Wizard said, tapping a pencil. "Whether it's letters of recommendation, evaluations, or ratings, there is frequently a tendency to use euphemisms that results in an unreal word picture of the person in question. When you've read enough of these things, you can begin to decipher what the intended meaning really is. Here are some descriptive words that have their own definition but may be used by a writer to convey another meaning. You have to look at the full text to get the real view. I'll alternate between the male pronoun and female pronoun for balance.

1. 'She's self-assured' could mean 'She has a constipated ego.'

2. 'He's respectful' could mean 'He thinks he knows how to impress people.'

3. 'She's loquacious' could mean 'She never shuts up.'

4. 'He's a risk taker' could mean 'He acts before he thinks.'

5. 'She's kind' could mean 'She's a soft touch.'

6. 'He's laid back' could mean 'They don't come any lazier.'

7. 'She's patient' could mean 'She's a schemer.'

8. 'He's adaptable' could mean 'He doesn't have any backbone.'

9. 'She's organized' could mean 'She's overly structured.'

10. 'He's eager' could mean 'He wades in where angels fear to tread.'

11. 'She's neighborly' could mean 'She never returns what she borrows.'

12. 'He's charming' could mean 'You'd better hold onto your wallet.'

13. 'She's attractive' could mean 'She's stuck on herself.'

14. 'He's expressive' could mean 'He gestures wildly.'

15. 'She's cheerful' could mean 'She's unrealistic.'

16. 'He's popular' could mean 'He knows the latest jokes.'

17. 'She possesses self-control' could mean 'She's uptight.'

18. 'He's optimistic' could mean 'He doesn't recognize facts.'

19. 'She's deliberate' could mean 'She's painfully slow.'

20. 'He's obedient' could mean 'He doesn't have a mind of his own.'

21. 'She's humble' could mean 'She plays that role to the hilt.'

22. 'He's a good listener' could mean 'He's always thinking of what he's going to say next.'

23. 'She's trustworthy' could mean 'She's naïve.'

24. 'He has character' could mean 'He is a character.'

25. 'She's a conformist' could mean 'She doesn't do anything innovative.'

26. 'He's tenacious' could mean 'He's an overbearing nuisance.'

27. 'She's receptive to new ideas' could mean 'She doesn't have any ideas of her own.'

28. 'He's independent' could mean 'He's not politically astute.'

29. 'She's a numbers-oriented person' could mean 'She has no personality.'

30. 'He's a people-oriented person' could mean 'He doesn't know numbers.'

31. 'She's vocal' could mean 'She talks a lot.'

32. 'He's competitive' could mean 'He doesn't play by the rules.'

33. 'She's even-tempered' could mean 'She doesn't make waves.'

34. 'He's assertive' could mean 'He's abrasively inflexible.'

35. 'She's logical' could mean 'She can find a million reasons not to do something.'

36. 'He commands respect' could mean 'He's a martinet.'

37. 'She's involved' could mean 'She's nosy.'

38. 'He's reliable' could mean 'He goes with the flow.'

39. 'She's a good communicator' could mean 'She sends a lot of e-mails to everyone.'

40. 'He's very persuasive' could mean 'He really talks a lot.'

41. 'She's very direct' could mean 'She tells it like she wants it to be.'

42. 'He's self-disciplined' could mean 'He never comes in early or stays late.'

43. 'She follows policies and procedures' could mean 'She can't see the forest for the trees.'

44. 'He's goal oriented' could mean 'He can't see the trees for the forest.'

45. 'She writes well' could mean 'She writes memos and memos and…'

46. 'He lends stability to the group' could mean 'He's a dragging anchor.'

47. 'She gets along well with others' could mean 'They tolerate her.'

48. 'He'll go the extra mile' could mean 'He likes to travel.'

49. 'She is exceptionally active' could mean 'She doesn't return phone calls.'

50. 'He looks for added responsibility' could mean 'He's never in his office.'

"Well, enough of this, Redael. You see the point," Winning Wizard concluded. "I'll sum it all up in

THE WIZARD'S WORDS OF MANAGEMENT WISDOM #56

Take written descriptions of others with a grain of pepper."

"Good play on words, Winning Wizard," said an amused Redael. "You hit the nail on the head, once again, from what I have experienced."

All-Star Team

"ARE YOU A FOOTBALL FAN, REDAEL?" Winning Wizard asked quizzically.

"As a matter of fact, I am, Winning Wizard. Why do you ask?" responded Redael.

"I've always felt that football is the recreational counterpart to an organizational environment, and I once wrote something as sort of an allegory that compares football positions with organizational positions. I put the organizational terms in parentheses. Want to hear it, Redael?" inquired Winning Wizard.

"Sure, I always like football stories," replied the football fan.

"O.K., Redael, consider the following positions," said Winning Wizard.

"**Quarterback (Chief Executive Officer)** is the keystone and pivotal position that determines all movement. The incumbent must have the game plan (vision and strategy) in mind well ahead of time (planning). The quarterback must be able to communicate clearly and forcefully issue the signals (directions) on which activity will commence, so that all team members, even wide receivers (branches) and linemen (lower echelons), can hear them. The quarterback must command the confidence and respect of teammates (employees), the opposition (competitors), and fans (customers). On the quarterback's shoulders rests the responsibility to score (achieve goals) and win (succeed). Quarterbacks have to be able to read the defense (the marketplace and competitors), have to be alert (quick-minded) to blitzes (surprise thrusts by competitors), and have to adjust by calling audibles (altering strategy in light of changed circumstances). They must be able to hand off (delegate), lateral (refer to staff), stay in the pocket (office) when necessary, scramble (visit the field) when required, and pass accurately (defer to others) when necessary or desirable. If they fumble (drop the ball) or are intercepted (miscalculate), they could be replaced. They must learn to play with pain (pressure), be eternally resilient (vibrant), and keep their team working together (coordinated) as a team (organization). They have to have clear vision (foresight) and natural ability (competency). They must call the right mix of plays (marketing/financial strategy) and use their personnel properly (select carefully and assess performance).

"**Running Backs (Operating Officers)** must be able to take the hand-off (directions) and advance the ball (programs) toward the end zone (company goals). They must be sure handed (have a good grip on matters) and not be prone to fumbling (committing errors). They have to be both strong (forceful) to pick up the short yardage (break through barriers) and nifty (have finesse) to slash (dart) through openings. They can't run off on their own (disrupt the system), and they have blocking responsibilities (mutual assistance). They must function as receivers (take assignments) when necessary.

"**Wide Receivers (Field Force)** must be swift (quick mental reflexes) because they are constantly in the defensive backfield (competitive marketplace). They must be able to report back (communicate) to the quarterback (CEO) what they think will work (suggestions) against the defense (competitive marketplace) when they return to the huddle (staff meetings). They must also be sure handed (have a grip on the situation) as they receive passes (assignments) from the quarterback (CEO). They have definite routes (policies) and patterns (procedures) to run (follow), and they must adhere to them (orderliness and discipline).

"**Offensive Line (Line Personnel)** are people who are in the trenches (on the firing line) and pave the way for progress on a consistent basis. They must be quick off the ball (on the ball) and be rugged (able to 'take it'). Every responsible quarterback (CEO) knows he or she would be sacked quickly (out) if it weren't for the linemen (line personnel). There is little glamour and publicity (public recognition), but morale must be good (sense of pride) at all times. If one falters (misses), others have to double up (cover). They must be able to take signals (take direction) and execute (perform) the play (according to the plan).

"**Head Coach (Chairman of the Board)** is available to the quarterback (CEO) for consultation at critical points. The coach receives reports from scouts (bankers, consultants) on the opposition (competitive marketplace). The coach reviews play selection (plans) of the quarterback (CEO) and assesses performance and may even send in plays (plans).

"**Assistant Coaches (Board Members)** provide counsel and advice in areas in which they specialize. Along with the head coach (Chairman), they comprise the coaching staff (the Board). They may not have any execution responsibilities (outside directors) or may be player coaches (inside directors).

"**Fans (Customers)** are often volatile and fickle. They pay their money and demand performance. They may not support the team (buy product or service) if expectations are not met with satisfaction, or they may switch allegiance to another (competitor) team (organization) if your performance is sloppy and you lose often. When you're winning (performing well), they can be great supporters (frequent customers) and make you the topic of conversation (word-of-mouth advertising).

"Well, there you have it, Redael. There are, of course, some differences between a football team and your team, I mean, your organization. Your people are not just Saturday's Heroes or Sunday's Heroes—they are Everyday's Heroes and Heroines. Allow me to kick off

THE WIZARD'S WORDS OF MANAGEMENT WISDOM #57

You have to let your people know constantly that in your eyes, they are your all-stars. If you don't, you could get sacked."

Recruiting the Best

"**A** GREAT MEASURE OF YOUR SUCCESS, REDAEL, will depend on the type of people with whom you surround yourself—that is to say, those people you recruit to come work with you," philosophized Winning Wizard. "So let's talk about the type of organization you want to run. Remember, Redael, we earlier determined that an 'organization' is a system of interrelationships between and among *people*.

"Some organizations are grossly inefficient and operate with limited, if any, effectiveness, which is readily apparent to the discerning eye. They are disorganized, which is worse than being unorganized. They exhibit an overall management sloppiness, slovenliness, lethargy, and laxity. An organizational laxative would help them. Other organizations convey an immediate rigidity, a sterile and distant atmosphere, a robotized procession of people mechanically performing their tasks, lacking spirit, zeal, and humor, and clothed with an overabundance of restrictive controls and narrow procedural channels to accomplish their objectives.

"You should strive for your organization to emit an instantaneous receptivity, not only to visitors but employee to employee, which translates into an interwoven vibrancy allowing for goal attainment assuredly and consistently. It's interesting to note the common elements that underpin the success of these progressive firms—success defined in both economic and human terms.

1. In recruiting and selecting key management personnel, successful executives choose the most qualified, competent, experienced or trainable, intellectually versatile, multitalented people they can identify. They choose people who can do a lot of things well. As a result they run lean in terms of number of staff. This aids productivity, of course. Their organizational strength is in their breadth of talent, not depth of staff. They offer top salaries, believing that this is the best investment they can make. Since their strength is not quantity but quality, their overall payroll is still in line. For these firms, the phrase 'catch the brightest stars' is more than an old reworked TV network slogan. The Chief Executive knows that hiring top talent is not a management panacea that will allow the reduction of managerial responsibility and time input. The management of highly spirited, multitalented people presents its own set of requirements for the CEO to master, but when the resources are there, the CEO has something with which to work.

2. Dynamic CEOs know that if the organization is to move forward, it's got to move up and move on. There is no room for the timid, the unsure, the 'avoid all risks' type in progressive organizations. This is not to say that there is recklessness, whimsy, or irresponsibility abounding; that caution is thrown to the wind; or that mistakes are not made. It is to say that, given deliberate and careful planning with attention focused on both short-term tactical and long-term strategic objectives, there is a pragmatic boldness, controlled aggressiveness, and quiet confidence that pervades the organization, which assists in meeting and overcoming the risks incurred.

3. It often has been suggested that good executives work smarter, not harder. That's only partly true. Top executives are smarter, which **causes** them to work harder toward mastery of the established objectives. As objectives expand in scope and magnitude, the successful executive works harder, gaining in expertise and advancing the organization. This process allows people to become more knowledgeable, which in turn allows them to work smarter. There is an ascending, self-reinforcing cycle of equal portions of keen intellect and physical effort that characterizes the employee force. An atmosphere of contribution to the organization exists among the employees. They give 110%

of themselves, which in itself is a source of pride to them. They truly manifest the work ethic. In less successful organizations, the atmosphere exuded by employees is often in the vein of 'I'll put forth the minimum effort. This place owes me something.'

4. A central principle that is evident to the naked eye in successful organizations is the acceptance of decisions, by top management, that are made at the level of impact where the decision will be felt, consistent with the overall mission and operating and administrative policies. Organizational superiors **don't normally** reverse decisions of subordinates when they have delegated authority to those subordinates for those types of decisions. Consequently, there is considerable dialogue and a noticeable absence of monologue. Differences of opinion are not looked on as one person or group being right and the others wrong but as a matter of preference or as arriving at different logical conclusions based on individual perception of the same set of facts and conditions. Decisions are made and directions are chosen, to be sure, but there is no individual or departmental destructive rivalry, ego strife, or 'one-upmanship' at play. Mutual trust, confidence, respect, and dedication among all employees is more than a byword in an orientation leaflet. It's practiced, and it's perfected.

"I think you see the point, Redael, so let me wrap up this discussion with

THE WIZARD'S WORDS OF MANAGEMENT WISDOM #58

The difference between serving people and processing people is sincerity. This applies to customers and employees alike. Recruit the best employees and you'll recruit the best customers. "

"I really do want to work in a good organization, Winning Wizard," said Redael hopefully. "I like living in this land of Yenom, and I want to be a productive employee and a productive citizen. I'll make it a point to be sincere when I deal with people."

The Management of
Tomorrow

"THOSE OF US WHO ARE IN THE SUNSET of our years, Redael, look with hope to those of you who are at the dawn of your careers," philosophized Winning Wizard. "You have limitless opportunity and potential kindled by your own vision and ambition."

"I sort of know that, Winning Wizard," said an anxious Redael. "But I do worry a little bit about the unknown."

"There will always be the unknown, Redael, but let me tell you what I see in your generation and possibly for generations to come.

"**A Sense of Significant Purpose.** Today's young managers seem to be happiest in an environment in which they have a sense of significant and measurable contribution to the known, and constantly reinforced purpose of the organization, and of their role in reaching that purpose. Your scope of personal concern encompasses not only your own and your organization's welfare but also the condition of society at large. You are more aware of national and world conditions than was true in the past. The world is not getting smaller—you have an expanded awareness.

"You want to feel that your working life is contributing not only to the organizational purpose, but that the organizational purpose itself is upstanding. In terms of contribution to the betterment of society, you want us to be on the leading edge because what we do is socially useful, economically developmental, and personally fulfilling. You want to be professional, and you want your organization to be professional. You are likely to ask, 'Where can I contribute most?' rather than 'What have you got to offer me?'

"**Growth Orientation.** Young managers are most excited in an organization that has a growth perspective both in terms of accelerated penetration into existing markets and the attraction of new markets and projects. What is interesting, however, is that this appeal is not only based on your potential advancement, which is assumed to some degree, but of equal importance is your enjoyment of the growth dynamics of setting direction, assembling resources, deploying resources according to plan, measuring progress, and achieving goals. You want to squeeze as much experience in as short a timeframe as possible. In a growth-oriented organization, promotion and financial advancement are taken somewhat for granted, and, therefore, young managers focus on operational challenges and the mental stimulation that accompanies them. You want to have faith in us, but sometimes you feel thwarted and isolated, not realizing others have the same pressures and problems. Some of us seniors apparently don't do a very good job of 'postsale marketing' with our employees. The growth perspective is based on a solid financial underpinning, and you want us to be an organization of substance. Young managers are drivers and strivers, aggressive and progressive, conscientious and unpretentious, energetic and kinetic. You are confident, curious, trusting, optimistic, and analytic. You also know you have a lot to learn, and you are simultaneously anxious and impatient. You could also be more creative.

"**Customer Perspective.** Young managers derive as much satisfaction from serving customers as you do from making budget and return on investment, although you worry that this is heresy to many of us. You are people oriented and represent the wave of youth who are revitalizing the service ethic. Generally speaking, you don't have the servitude hangup that was evident some years back or is characteristic of those who are insecure. You delight in serving people, believing that it is the **right** thing to do. In this regard, you have a generalized unselfishness. You are genuine, cordial, and sincere in your relations with others. You are also somewhat naïve, however, having grown up in an abundant environment. You really haven't tasted failure, and scarcity hasn't touched you. Inflation is viewed as relative and is something you read about. You tend to be overly trusting.

"A **Positive Internal Climate.** Another thread in the emerging management fabric is the desire of young managers to operate in a positive internal climate, wherein your thoughts are not disrespected because of your age and you are not suspected because of your education. You like to be judged on performance, not seniority, and you like to be given responsibility, not assigned only minor tasks. You need reminding from time to time that you are a definite resource to the organization, and you want to feel that we provide a measure of loyalty to you equal to that you give to us. You want to be more than just on the team. You want to be in the game. You also want us to recognize that you want to live a quality life in all that you do.

"**Principle, Ethics, and Quality.** Young managers are mindful of good business practices, organizational codes of ethics, and the quality level of the product and/or service of the organization. You are repulsed by violations in the name of expediency and short-term profit and recoil at decisions that are made on a nonobjective basis. You have a longer-term view, as well as a global view, and seek solid answers to valid questions beyond 'it's company policy.' You have a social security number, an employee identification number, a driver's license number, a license plate number, a telephone number, several credit card numbers, and perhaps a locker number. You also have some flesh, some blood, and a mind that you want to use. You think of yourself as a high-quality person who has something to offer, and you want to work with quality, and provide quality, in everything you do. You want to prepare for the future, and you need to feel you are **being prepared** for the future. You want to believe that the best of everything you will ever know is still ahead of you.

"Well, Redael, let me sum up because it's time for

THE WIZARD'S WORDS OF MANAGEMENT WISDOM #59

The management of tomorrow will only be as good as the management of today allows it to be."

"I think you'll be seeing a few more sunsets and sunrises, Winning Wizard," Redael said with emotion. "We look to people such as you to mold us and guide us into the future."

The Perfect Executive

"WELL, REDAEL, WE'VE HAD QUITE a conversation," sighed Winning Wizard, "and I've enjoyed it immensely."

"We most certainly have, Winning Wizard, and I have received more insights and provocative thoughts than I ever imagined," Redael stated with an air of finality and appreciation. "I've taken copious notes, and I'll digest them and refer to them time and time again, I'm sure."

"I'm glad you feel our time together has been beneficial Redael, but I feel the need to come to complete closure to give you take-away value for the investment of time you've made with me," Winning Wizard said. "Let me tell you about 'the Perfect Executive' now that you are aware of all we have discussed."

"Good!" exclaimed Redael, "I'd like your closing thoughts."

"First of all, my young friend, we need to recognize that perfection is a value, not an object. Therefore, it's not wholly measurable quantitatively. Most of us recognize it, however, when we experience it. Here are 60 qualities that I feel are the components of 'the Perfect Executive.' Mark them well, Redael," advised Winning Wizard.

"The Perfect Executive possesses the following:

1. The **curiosity** of a cat
2. The **tenacity** of a bulldog
3. The **pride** of a peacock
4. The **humility** of a monk
5. The **eagerness** of a student
6. The **wisdom** of a professor
7. The **hope** of an optimist
8. The **courage** of a champion
9. The **dynamism** of a perpetual motion machine
10. The **patience** of Job
11. The **memory** of an elephant
12. The **understanding** of a parent
13. The **skin** of a rhinoceros
14. The **sensitivity** of a teenager
15. The **discipline** of a ballerina
16. The **adaptability** of a chameleon
17. The **work ethic** of a beaver
18. The **service ethic** of a cleric
19. The **endurance** of a long-distance runner
20. The **pace** of a sprinter
21. The **thriftiness** of a Scotsman
22. The **generosity** of a benefactor
23. The **poise** of a diplomat
24. The **perspective** of a statesman or stateswoman
25. The **vision** of a builder
26. The **confidence** of an achiever
27. The **respect** of a queen bee
28. The **sense of humor** of a comic
29. The **organizational ability** of a spider
30. The **creativity** of an artist
31. The **dedication** of an Olympic athlete

32. The **trust** of a friend

33. The **persuasiveness** of an automobile salesperson

34. The **inspiration** of a coach

35. The **resiliency** of a rubber ball

36. The **stability** of the Rock of Gibraltar

37. The **judgment** of an umpire

38. The **ambition** of an ant

39. The **integrity** of a judge

40. The **objectivity** of a scientist

41. The **motivation** of a treasure hunter

42. The **alertness** of a fox

43. The **analytical ability** of a computer

44. The **communication ability** of a crusader

45. The **standards** of a university president

46. The **goal orientation** of a hockey player

47. The **reliability** of a tax assessor

48. The **heart** of a lion

49. The **intellect** of Socrates

50. The **focus** of a jeweler

51. The **speaking ability** of a champion debater

52. The **writing ability** of a Pulitzer prize winner

53. The **listening ability** of a psychiatrist

54. The **resolve** of a medical researcher

55. The **toughness** of tempered steel

56. The **growth orientation** of a landscaper

57. The **enthusiasm** of a cheerleader

58. The **logic** of a mathematician

59. The **luck** of a lottery winner

60. The **spirit** of a person of accomplishment

"And so, my friend, these are Winning Wizard's final Words of Management Wisdom, at least for this discussion:

The Wizard's Words of Management Wisdom #60

The perfect executive is _____ (Fill in your name at the appropriate point in your managerial maturity.)"

"I may never be perfect, Winning Wizard, but I'm going to try to come as close to it as anyone ever has," pledged Redael. "I've got to go now, Winning Wizard, and I'm going to put into practice what you have said."

Epilogue

WINNING WIZARD LEANED BACK in the soft leather chair behind the large Chippendale desk and reflected on the conversation with the eager young trainee. "Redael certainly seemed interested and alert and took copious notes," the mentor thought, "but I wonder if I really got through with the insights I wanted to convey."

"Redael is young," Winning Wizard muttered, "and will face a lot in the future. I probably should have offered a final piece of advice, for this conversation anyway. I should have mentioned

THE WIZARD'S WORDS OF MANAGEMENT WISDOM #61

Organizational life is full of surprises, but you must never act surprised.

"Perhaps there will be another occasion when Redael and I will have another conversation." the mentor thought with a trace of hope. "Perhaps we will talk again. Perhaps . . ."

Over the next several months, Redael reflected on the points Winning Wizard had made during the conversation. A number of situations did arise that Redael recognized as the result of the tutorial and that were managed adeptly using Winning Wizard's perspective. On other occasions, Redael did not handle things all that well, and only after the fact, when there was time to digest and analyze what occurred, did Redael realize that a lot of what the mentor said could have been applied, which would have led to a different outcome. "I guess I'm learning through experience," Redael thought.

Six months after meeting with Winning Wizard, some organizational changes resulted in a surprise promotion for Redael. "Wow, this is a surprising development," Redael thought. "I have more responsibility, and I'm beginning to ascend the organizational mountain Winning Wizard told me about. There is more I could learn, I'm sure. I should give Winning Wizard a call to announce my new assignment and perhaps make another appointment," Redael thought. "Perhaps I'll do that. Perhaps . . ."

Index

Environment, organizational,
88–90
Equality, 37
Equilibrium, 124
Equity, 37
Essentiality, 123–124
Ethics, 136
Excellence, 56, 123
Expertise authority, 25
Extroversion, 57

F

Field force, 129
Formal groups, 78

G

Groups
assembling, 82
behavior, 82–85
characteristics, 78–80
control, 102
definition, 77–78
effectiveness, 85
forming, 78
function, 83
leaders and, 83–84
setting, 82–84
structure, 84–85
symbols, 85
types, 78
Growth orientation, 135

H

Hooke, Robert, 49
Human resources, 16
Humor, 57

I

Identification authority, 25
Informal groups, 78
Intelligence, 10, 55–56
Intent theory, 52
Inventiveness, 109
Involuntary groups, 78

K

Knowledge, 74–76

L

Leadership. *See also* Chief executive
officers; Managers
angelic style, 66–69
aspects, 52
in bureaucracy, 95–98
definition, 51, 53–54
direction of, 48
groups, 54, 83–84
imperial style, 59–61
individual, 53
knowledgeable, 74–76
loyalty, 76
pragmatic style, 70–73
qualities, 59–61
situations, 87–91
theories, 51–52
traits, 55–58
virtues, 117–121
Le Chatelier, 49
Legal authority, 25
Line personnel, 129–130
Loyalty, 76

M

Managers
attributes, 6–7
consistence, 15–17
future of, 134–136
vices, 7–8
Means, organizational, 28
Mixers, 45

N

Newton, Isaac, 47–48

O

Obsessions, 18–20
Open door policy, 99–101
Operating officers, 129
Organizations
abstraction, 33–35
competition, 40–42
conflicts, 27–29
controls, 102–104
environments, 88–90
ethics, 136

Leadership Axioms
for
Career Progression
and Everyday Living

WILLIAM P. FISHER, PH.D.
CHRISTOPHER C. MULLER, PH.D.

THOMSON

DELMAR LEARNING

Australia Canada Mexico Singapore Spain United Kingdom United States

THOMSON

DELMAR LEARNING

Winning Wizard's Leadership Axioms
for Career Progression and Everyday Living

William P. Fisher, Ph.D.
Christopher C. Muller, Ph.D.

Vice President, Career Education SBU:
Dawn Gerrain

Director of Learning Solutions:
Sherry Gomoll

Managing Editor:
Robert L. Serenka, Jr.

Acquisitions Editor:
Martine Edwards

Editorial Assistant:
Jennifer Anderson

Director of Production:
Wendy A. Troeger

Production Manager:
J.P. Henkel

Production Editor:
Rebecca Goldthwaite

Director of Marketing:
Wendy E. Mapstone

Channel Manager:
Gerard McAvey

Marketing Coordinator:
Erica Conley

Cover & Text Design:
essence of 7

NOTICE TO THE READER

Preface

A colleague of ours, to whom we gave the manuscript to read for review and comment, asked us, "How long did it take you to write this book?" Bill Fisher answered "65 years!" Chris Muller answered "51 years!"

Our colleague registered momentary surprise but quickly caught the significance of the responses. People are not "born" leaders in the sense that they have "LEADER" printed on their foreheads (or behinds, as the case may be) at their moment of birth. Leadership is a learning process, and as with any such activity both successes and errors occur. It is through the assimilation of sequential experiences that leadership concepts—or axioms, as we call them—take root, germinate, and flower.

The impetus for the book crystallized when the two of us co-developed a new course on leadership that we co-teach. Both of us have creative minds (we think and have been so told), and we decided to visually open each class with a "leadership axiom" that the students could read, copy, ingest, contemplate, and remember if so desired. As we began to put our thoughts on paper, both of us drew from our own experiences in leadership positions and from observations of others in leadership positions. We decided to stop at 417 (far, far exceeding the number of classes in a semester—30) but felt the need to codify what our experiences, observations, and imaginations compelled us to document.

We purposely have termed each insight an "axiom" because the definition of that word includes (among other things) "a universal proposition, amply proved, easily verifiable, or generally accepted" (*New American Webster Handy College Dictionary*). Our axioms fit this definition perfectly. We suggest that there is an "axiom a day" contained herein that you, the reader, can take to heart without being overwhelmed (or underwhelmed) by multiple thoughts at one time.

We made one exception, however! Because a lot of people have a "case of the Mondays" we suggest reading two axioms on Mondays, so you can be doubly inspired to start off the week at an accelerating speed. That's why we stopped at 417 (365 + 52 = 417). The wisdom contained herein is invaluable.

We hope you enjoy it, but more importantly, we hope you benefit from it.

Christopher C. Muller, Ph.D.   William P. Fisher, Ph.D.

Tenured Professor   Darden Eminent Scholar Chair

Dedication

The authors wish to dedicate this lasting memorial to their families— past, present, and future:

The members of the Fisher family

The members of the Muller family

(*Note:* The authors are perpetually perplexed as to why the members of the families of leaders don't consider them to be leaders of the family. Perhaps it's a paradox of human nature.)

We also want to dedicate this book to current and aspiring leaders of all ages and in all walks of life!

Appreciation

The authors wish to thank our professional colleagues for their insight; our students for their foresight; and in particular, Mr. Gregory Good for his assistance (and tolerance).

About the Authors

W illiam P. Fisher, Ph.D., is the Darden Eminent Scholar Chair in restaurant management in the Rosen College of Hospitality Management at the University of Central Florida in Orlando. He previously held positions as the chief executive officer of the American Hotel & Lodging Association and the National Restaurant Association, both based in Washington, D.C. He also was the executive vice president of finance and administration for a major food service contract management organization.

He holds three degrees from Cornell University: a B.S. in hotel administration, an M.B.A. (finance), and a Ph.D. in educational administration.

His academic credentials include service as an assistant professor in the school of hotel administration, where he taught accounting, finance, and management courses. He was a partner in the consulting firm of Gaurnier Associates simultaneously with his teaching responsibilities.

The author of numerous articles and books, Dr. Fisher was recognized as "Champion of Education" by the Council on Hotel, Restaurant, and Institutional Education (CHRIE) in 1996, and is the first recipient of the Michael E. Hurst Lifetime Achievement in Education Award, bestowed by the Education Foundation of the National Restaurant Association.

Married for more than 40 years, he and his wife, Yvonne, have three children and nine grandchildren.

Christopher Muller earned his doctorate and master's degrees from Cornell University, and his bachelor's degree from Hobart College. He is currently a professor in the Rosen College of Hospitality Management in Orlando, Forida where he is the director of the Center for Multi-Unit Restaurant Management. Muller is the president and founder of a start-up casual service restaurant company, 'Za-Bistro!, based in Maitland, Florida. He has lectured extensively on service, management, and leadership to companies and organizations around the world. He is also the co-author, with Bill Fisher, of *Four-Dimensional Leadership: The Individual; The Lifecycle; The Organization; The Community*, and *Leadership Exercises! Taking a Leadership Role in the Hospitality Industry*.

Prologue

Winning Wizard is a successful executive, now retired, who remains as a Chief Executive Officer Emeritus of the organization that was the beneficiary of so many years of tireless and dedicated service. Redael, a young management trainee and now a junior executive, was referred to Winning Wizard to receive some "words of wisdom" when no one else in the organization would take the time to counsel the fledging young employee. Winning Wizard thus became a mentor to Redael and considerable "wisdom" was dispensed to the eager young listener. This portfolio of counsel is contained in two publications entitled *Winning Wizard's Words of Management Wisdom—Starting Out*, and *Winning Wizard's Words of Management Wisdom—Moving Up*. Redael found the wisdom of Winning Wizard to be enormously interesting and useful, and now as a junior executive ready to ascend to the ranks of senior management, Redael feels a need to speak with the sage once again. We start from this point.

Introduction

"Now that I have been told I am being groomed for a senior management position, I should give Winning Wizard a call and have another conversation," Redael thought, somewhat resolutely. "I know upper management positions carry leadership responsibilities and Winning Wizard could probably give me a lot of good pointers that could prove valuable for my future."

"I see that my young friend, Redael, will be promoted soon to a higher level office in our organization," Winning Wizard ruminated. "I think my earlier words of management wisdom have been helpful in this regard, but I should probably share some thoughts on the subject of leadership to help develop a leadership mindset and daily guide," mused the mentor.

The telephone rang in Winning Wizard's office in the Stratospheric Lounge, and the CEO Emeritus picked it up on the third chime. "Hello, Redael," said the mentor. "I was just thinking about you."

"I forgot you had caller identification, Winning Wizard, so you knew it was me, didn't you?" said a maturing Redael.

"Yes, I did, actually," Winning Wizard confirmed, "and I am delighted to hear from you. I understand some good news may be headed your way. Would you like to have another conversation?"

"That's the reason for the call, Winning Wizard. Can we arrange a mutually convenient time to get together?" the young executive inquired.

"Of course we can, Redael, of course we can. Let's check our calendars," the sage intoned, looking forward to the meeting.

Winning Wizard rose from the cushioned leather chair behind the desk as Redael entered the office and the two generations greeted one another with doubled hand clasps. "Welcome, Redael. It's nice to see you looking so poised and prosperous. Your career must agree with you in this land of Yenom," complimented Winning Wizard.

"Thank you, Winning Wizard, and I can say that you have not changed a bit. You still have that leadership demeanor and air of command," Redael retorted, returning one compliment with another. "That's the reason I am here, Winning Wizard, to receive from you some pointers on the subject of leadership, which I know I will have to have as I ascend the organizational ladder," Redael stated with anticipation.

"Leadership is a vast subject, Redael. Volumes have been written about it, and it still continues to be an enigma for many people," Winning Wizard stated. "I do have some thoughts that may be helpful to you, though, 417 of them to be exact. Can you handle that many?"

"I believe I can, Winning Wizard, but 417 is an unusual number. How did you arrive at that total?" Redael asked.

"Early in my career, Redael, I felt I should write down my thoughts on leadership as I experienced or observed different situations. One day I codified them, and I assembled them into one for every day of the year, which is 365, as you know." A broad smile swept across Winning Wizard's face. "However, on Mondays I felt the need for a little extra leadership energy, so I added 52 more, one additional for each Monday, and that's how I reached 417," the mentor exclaimed. "You may want to look at them in this light as well."

"Wow! I can't wait, Winning Wizard. May we get started?" said Redael.

"Sure we can, Redael. I call them *Winning Wizard's Leadership Axioms*," noted the teacher. "Here we go!"

LEADERSHIP AXIOM #1

Successful leadership is:
20% Vision
20% Courage
20% Persona
20% Timing
20% Luck

LEADERSHIP AXIOM #2

Leadership is founded on preparation and opportunity.

LEADERSHIP AXIOM #3

Leadership is not forged in tranquility; it is forged in adversity.

LEADERSHIP AXIOM #4

The absence of leadership creates anxiety and decay.
The presence of leadership creates confidence and spirit.

LEADERSHIP AXIOM #5

The function of leadership is not to get others to favor you,
but to get others to follow you.

LEADERSHIP AXIOM #6

If you want to develop the virtues and qualities to become
a leader, act as though you already possess them.

LEADERSHIP AXIOM #7

*The only thing more dispiriting than inept followers
is inept leadership.*

LEADERSHIP AXIOM #8

*The ultimate test of leaders is that they prepare successors
who surpass themselves.*

LEADERSHIP AXIOM #9

*Some organizations are transformed by the individuals who lead them.
Some organizations transcend the individuals who purport
to lead them.*

LEADERSHIP AXIOM #10

Good leaders lead leading organizations.
Leading organizations develop good leaders.

LEADERSHIP AXIOM #11

Organizations abhor a leadership vacuum.

LEADERSHIP AXIOM #12

Leadership is not an honorary position.

LEADERSHIP AXIOM #13

True leaders change lives…for the better.

LEADERSHIP AXIOM #14

Paradoxically, leaders know that there are times when it's "wrong" to be right (diplomacy).

LEADERSHIP AXIOM #15

Leadership is not always taking others where they want to go; it's taking them where they need to go.

LEADERSHIP AXIOM #16

Leaders know that "the dog who never leaves the porch will never find a bone."

LEADERSHIP AXIOM #17

Leaders "always put their best jockey on their fastest horse."

LEADERSHIP AXIOM #18

Leaders know that confidence is internal mastery, and effectiveness is external mastery.

LEADERSHIP AXIOM #19

Leaders know that it is relatively easy to mend a broken bone, but it's quite something else to mend a broken spirit.

LEADERSHIP AXIOM #20

A true leader is not above the team, just the head of it.

LEADERSHIP AXIOM #21

Leaders make things happen. Some others watch what happens. Most others wonder what happened.

LEADERSHIP AXIOM #22

*Leaders know that the only time you can coast
is when you are going downhill.*

LEADERSHIP AXIOM #23

*Leaders know that it is not what lies behind you that is important,
nor is it what lies ahead of you that is important.
It's what lies within you that is most important.*

LEADERSHIP AXIOM #24

*Leaders know they can't see the whole picture
when they are inside the frame.*

LEADERSHIP AXIOM #25

Leaders know there are two types of training: deficiency training and development training. Leaders emphasize the latter.

LEADERSHIP AXIOM #26

Leaders know that when the group is coming from nowhere there are lots of places to go.

LEADERSHIP AXIOM #27

A leader is a dream maker and a goal achiever.

LEADERSHIP AXIOM #28

Leaders know that behind big problems lie big opportunities.

LEADERSHIP AXIOM #29

Leaders know that experience is the best teacher.
It gives you the test first, and then you learn the lesson.

LEADERSHIP AXIOM #30

Leaders know that genius is 1% inspiration and 99% perspiration.

LEADERSHIP AXIOM #31

*Leaders know that they can't make a good deal with bad people,
and they can't make a bad deal with good people.*

LEADERSHIP AXIOM #32

*Leaders think and act with a cool head and a warm heart,
not with a hot head and a cold heart.*

LEADERSHIP AXIOM #33

Leaders know there is a great risk in not taking a chance.

LEADERSHIP AXIOM #34

*Leaders know that one of the most difficult aspects of their role
is telling others they will not realize their dreams.*

LEADERSHIP AXIOM #35

*Leaders know that good judgment comes from experience
and that experience comes from poor judgment.*

LEADERSHIP AXIOM #36

Leaders know that the lead horse always has the best view.

LEADERSHIP AXIOM #37

Leaders know that their reputation is what the world thinks of them.
They also know that character is what they think of themselves.

LEADERSHIP AXIOM #38

When leaders win, they don't boast. When they don't win, they don't cry.

LEADERSHIP AXIOM #39

Leaders know that they need to stand for something
or their followers could fall for anything.

LEADERSHIP AXIOM #40

*Leaders don't let early successes stunt their growth.
Neither do they let early failures erode their spirit.*

LEADERSHIP AXIOM #41

*Leaders know they need to be mentally tough
or they could become emotionally scarred.*

LEADERSHIP AXIOM #42

*Leaders know that they are exemplars,
held to higher-than-average standards.*

Leadership Axiom #43

Leaders know that achievement is a journey, not a destination.

Leadership Axiom #44

Leaders know that strong discipline can be a great kindness in the long run.

Leadership Axiom #45

Leaders know that some things are unwritten and unspoken but are clearly understood by all.

LEADERSHIP AXIOM #46

Leaders know they must give their followers roots,
but they must also give them wings.

LEADERSHIP AXIOM #47

Leaders know that half of everything is below average.

LEADERSHIP AXIOM #48

Leaders know that if they are not part of the solution,
they are part of the problem.

LEADERSHIP AXIOM #49

*Leaders have a touch of an athlete's timing, a gambler's nerve,
a magician's tricks, and a diplomat's poise.*

LEADERSHIP AXIOM #50

*A leader knows that when he or she gives a child a hammer,
the whole world becomes a nail.*

LEADERSHIP AXIOM #51

*Leaders know that one moment of irresponsibility can produce
a lifetime of regret.*

LEADERSHIP AXIOM #52

*Leaders know that if they always do what they always did,
they will always get what they always got.*

LEADERSHIP AXIOM #53

*Leaders know that sometimes they may have to bash heads
for minds to meet.*

LEADERSHIP AXIOM #54

Leaders don't make the same mistake twice.

LEADERSHIP AXIOM #55

*Leaders know that it is thunder that roars,
but it's lightning that strikes.*

LEADERSHIP AXIOM #56

People appreciate quiet leaders. Loud leaders lack grace and humility.

LEADERSHIP AXIOM #57

You need to train to be a good leader to reign as a good leader.

LEADERSHIP AXIOM #58

One who leads last leads best.

LEADERSHIP AXIOM #59

Great leaders are like great art. They stand the test of time.

LEADERSHIP AXIOM #60

Leaders know that correlation is not causation.

LEADERSHIP AXIOM #61

The coefficient of leadership is service.

LEADERSHIP AXIOM #62

Leaders do what they can do for those who can't.

LEADERSHIP AXIOM #63

Leaders learn from the past, act in the present, and plan for the future.

LEADERSHIP AXIOM #64

Leaders teach—they don't preach.

LEADERSHIP AXIOM #65

When leaders care about their people, their people care about them.

LEADERSHIP AXIOM #66

Leadership is a lifestyle.

LEADERSHIP AXIOM #67

Leaders pay their dues—
D*edication,* **U***nderstanding,* **E***nergy,* **S***tandards.*

LEADERSHIP AXIOM #68

Leadership is a 24/7 position.

LEADERSHIP AXIOM #69

Leaders don't let criticism bother them. Criticism bolsters them.

Leadership Axiom #70

Leadership is part art and part science. It emerges from the inside but is developed by the outside.

Leadership Axiom #71

Followers support leaders who support them.

Leadership Axiom #72

Leaders are never tentative. They are always affirmative.

LEADERSHIP AXIOM #73

The greatest tribute to a leader is not adulation, it's accomplishment.

LEADERSHIP AXIOM #74

Leaders don't just have the gift of sight—they have the gift of vision.

LEADERSHIP AXIOM #75

Leaders are gracious, never ingratiating.

LEADERSHIP AXIOM #76

True leaders never give in, nor do they give up.

LEADERSHIP AXIOM #77

Leaders know you don't have to be a sinner to be a winner.

LEADERSHIP AXIOM #78

Before they engineer success, leaders imagineer *success.*

LEADERSHIP AXIOM #79

True leaders are not sprinters—they are long distance runners.

LEADERSHIP AXIOM #80

Leaders don't pass the buck—they invest it.

LEADERSHIP AXIOM #81

Leaders are quadrisighted—they have hindsight, foresight, insight, and oversight.

LEADERSHIP AXIOM #82

Leaders don't just hear—they listen.

LEADERSHIP AXIOM #83

Leaders don't just see things—they can see through things.

LEADERSHIP AXIOM #84

Leaders speak both artfully and articulately.

LEADERSHIP AXIOM #85

Leaders write not only incisively but also decisively.

LEADERSHIP AXIOM #86

Leaders have power:
Poise, **O**rganization, **W**isdom, **E**nthusiasm, **R**esponsibility.

LEADERSHIP AXIOM #87

A good leader is a follower...of his or her conscience.

LEADERSHIP AXIOM #88

*The best time to become a leader is when there is a need
and a vacuum.*

LEADERSHIP AXIOM #89

Leaders act out of inspiration, not desperation.

LEADERSHIP AXIOM #90

Leaders do not shrink from rational risk—they rise to conquer it.

LEADERSHIP AXIOM #91

Leaders are not really lonely at the top—they are lively at the top.

LEADERSHIP AXIOM #92

Leadership is a quality, not a quantity.

LEADERSHIP AXIOM #93

Followers follow on the basis of perception and faith.
Leaders confirm both.

LEADERSHIP AXIOM #94

The times can make the leader. The leader can also make the times.

LEADERSHIP AXIOM #95

Leaders today were readers yesterday.

LEADERSHIP AXIOM #96

Leaders are not self-conscious. They are self-confident.

LEADERSHIP AXIOM #97

Leaders are detail conscious, but they are not detail confined.

LEADERSHIP AXIOM #98

Leaders are mentors to their people, not tormentors of their people.

LEADERSHIP AXIOM #99

Leaders know they don't have all the answers.
They also know they don't have all the questions.

LEADERSHIP AXIOM #100

True leaders are not egocentric—they are sociocentric.

LEADERSHIP AXIOM #101

Leaders at any level are CEOs: **C***aring,* **E***ffective,* **O***rganized.*

LEADERSHIP AXIOM #102

Leaders know that the best discipline of all is self-discipline.

LEADERSHIP AXIOM #103

Leaders know that when dealing with people and property there is only one type of honesty—total. Any deviance from total honesty is some measure of dishonesty.

LEADERSHIP AXIOM #104

Leaders exude and encourage an improvement attitude.

LEADERSHIP AXIOM #105

Leaders know they must give respect to receive respect.

LEADERSHIP AXIOM #106

Leaders regard setbacks as temporary.

LEADERSHIP AXIOM #107

Leaders know that the best control is self-control.

LEADERSHIP AXIOM #108

Leaders think with their heads, not with their hearts.

LEADERSHIP AXIOM #109

Leaders are assertive, not acerbic.

LEADERSHIP AXIOM #110

Leaders have a sense of humor and also a sense of humility.

LEADERSHIP AXIOM #111

Leaders share accomplishments with their people.

LEADERSHIP AXIOM #112

When events overwhelm others, leaders overwhelm the events.

LEADERSHIP AXIOM #113

Leaders know the difference between equality and equity.
The former is spiritually and politically based,
and the latter is performance and results based.

LEADERSHIP AXIOM #114

Leaders look for remedies, not blame.

LEADERSHIP AXIOM #115

Leaders look to involve themselves, not absolve themselves.

LEADERSHIP AXIOM #116

Leaders have goals: **G***ood* **O***rganizational* **A***nd* **L***anguage* **S***kills.*

LEADERSHIP AXIOM #117

Leaders are not clock watchers. They are performance watchers.

LEADERSHIP AXIOM #118

*Leaders know that the rightful use of authority
is to serve those who have granted it.*

LEADERSHIP AXIOM #119

Leaders cultivate trust:
Truth, **R**esponsibility, **U**nderstanding, **S**tability, **T**enacity.

LEADERSHIP AXIOM #120

Leaders are good navigators. They are also good negotiators.

LEADERSHIP AXIOM #121

Leaders are complimentary to their people, not caustic to them.

LEADERSHIP AXIOM #122

Leaders treat their people with dignity, not with disdain.

LEADERSHIP AXIOM #123

Leaders can affect eternity.
You can't calculate where their influence stops.

LEADERSHIP AXIOM #124

Leaders possess a lot of fight:
Fidelity, **I**ntegrity, **G**umption, **H**onor, **T**rustworthiness.

LEADERSHIP AXIOM #125

Leaders are tenacious, not tentative.

LEADERSHIP AXIOM #126

Leaders develop their people, they don't envelop them.

LEADERSHIP AXIOM #127

Leaders know the best evaluation of all is self-evaluation.

LEADERSHIP AXIOM #128

Leaders are objective, but they are not insensitive.

LEADERSHIP AXIOM #129

Leaders believe in the three Cs: Courage, Confidence, Competence.

LEADERSHIP AXIOM #130

Leaders can adapt with agility and alacrity.

LEADERSHIP AXIOM #131

*Leaders talk the talk, walk the walk, measure the measures,
and praise people.*

LEADERSHIP AXIOM #132

Leaders are constructively critical, not hypocritical.

LEADERSHIP AXIOM #133

Leaders weigh their words, and their words are weighed.

LEADERSHIP AXIOM #134

Leaders don't avoid risk—they manage risk.

LEADERSHIP AXIOM #135

Leaders overcome frustration with determination.

LEADERSHIP AXIOM #136

Leaders know that the most important thing they wear is their smile.

LEADERSHIP AXIOM #137

Leaders know the difference between demanding and commanding.
The former is dictatorial, and the latter is organizational.

LEADERSHIP AXIOM #138

Leaders work hard. They also work smart.

LEADERSHIP AXIOM #139

Leaders seek to be inclusive, not exclusive.

LEADERSHIP AXIOM #140

*Leaders don't just want their organizations to survive—
they want their organizations to thrive.*

LEADERSHIP AXIOM #141

Leaders go for "the win," not "the tie."

LEADERSHIP AXIOM #142

The only excess leaders allow themselves is success.

LEADERSHIP AXIOM #143

Leaders don't relegate—they delegate.

LEADERSHIP AXIOM #144

Leaders are consistent, not just insistent.

LEADERSHIP AXIOM #145

Leaders stand behind their people. They also stand in front of them.

LEADERSHIP AXIOM #146

Leaders don't just speed read, they speed think.

LEADERSHIP AXIOM #147

Leaders don't just ingest information—they digest it.

LEADERSHIP AXIOM #148

Leadership is a mindset and a bodyset.

LEADERSHIP AXIOM #149

*Leaders know they must focus on a balanced life
as well as their balance sheet.*

LEADERSHIP AXIOM #150

The leader's principal principle is to serve others.

LEADERSHIP AXIOM #151

Leaders are more than utilitarians. They are possibilitarians.

LEADERSHIP AXIOM #152

True leaders captivate the minds, hearts, and souls of their followers.

LEADERSHIP AXIOM #153

Leaders don't allow themselves to get depressed.
They allow themselves to get refreshed.

LEADERSHIP AXIOM #154

Leaders know their most enduring asset is their reputation.

LEADERSHIP AXIOM #155

Positionship is not leadership. The former is an organizational depiction. The latter is constituent acceptance.

LEADERSHIP AXIOM #156

Leaders know that it is easy to criticize when you don't have the responsibility. They still take the responsibility.

LEADERSHIP AXIOM #157

Leaders don't just do things right—they do the right things.

LEADERSHIP AXIOM #158

Leaders are effervescent, not quiescent.

LEADERSHIP AXIOM #159

Leaders not only advocate teamwork—they advocate teamthink.

LEADERSHIP AXIOM #160

Leaders are the architects of the organization's culture.

LEADERSHIP AXIOM #161

True leaders are human. True leaders are also humane.

LEADERSHIP AXIOM #162

Leaders, by nature, are optimistic. They are also realistic.

LEADERSHIP AXIOM #163

Leaders can often signal their thoughts through silence.

LEADERSHIP AXIOM #164

Leaders are discreet in the display of their intelligence.

LEADERSHIP AXIOM #165

Leaders cultivate their organizational culture.

LEADERSHIP AXIOM #166

Leaders encourage both creativity and conformity.

LEADERSHIP AXIOM #167

Leaders respect the chain of command.

LEADERSHIP AXIOM #168

Leaders don't despair—they repair.

LEADERSHIP AXIOM #169

Leaders convert a "can do" demeanor into a "can did" result.

LEADERSHIP AXIOM #170

Coercion is not leadership, it is domination.

LEADERSHIP AXIOM #171

The five leadership senses (not physical senses):
Vision, Articulation, Radiation, Empathy, Common.

LEADERSHIP AXIOM #172

Leaders know that authority is a tool, not a weapon.

LEADERSHIP AXIOM #173

*Leaders know that they can delegate authority
but they can't delegate responsibility.*

LEADERSHIP AXIOM #174

Leaders don't just put in their time—they put more into their time.

LEADERSHIP AXIOM #175

Leaders can do two things at once as long as one thing is passive and the other is active.

LEADERSHIP AXIOM #176

Strong leaders are strong motivators.

LEADERSHIP AXIOM #177

True leaders don't bask in their press clippings.

LEADERSHIP AXIOM #178

Leaders **conceive** *of themselves as leaders,* **carry** *themselves as leaders, and* **conduct** *themselves as leaders.*

LEADERSHIP AXIOM #179

Leaders have a mission: **M**aturity, **I**nnovation, **S**tability, **S**trength, **I**ntuition, **O**rganization, **N**obility.

LEADERSHIP AXIOM #180

Leaders know that ordinary minds talk about people.
Extraordinary minds talk about ideas.

LEADERSHIP AXIOM #181

The fundamental basis for leadership is to have followers.

LEADERSHIP AXIOM #182

Leaders build and solidify the organization's identity.

LEADERSHIP AXIOM #183

*Leaders know that one of their functions
is to be the organization's head "cheerleader."*

LEADERSHIP AXIOM #184

Leaders not only clean their bodies on a routine basis—
they also clean their minds on a routine basis.

LEADERSHIP AXIOM #185

Leaders don't destroy resources—they deploy resources.

LEADERSHIP AXIOM #186

Leaders live their lives in the primary form.
They are not "virtual" in any respect.

LEADERSHIP AXIOM #199

Leaders wear the cloak of command well.

LEADERSHIP AXIOM #200

Leaders accept the mantle of their office.

LEADERSHIP AXIOM #201

Leaders evidence a trust in others, but they still look for verification.

LEADERSHIP AXIOM #202

Leaders have a competitive core. They also have a compassionate core.

LEADERSHIP AXIOM #203

Leaders accept being cussed and discussed because they are focused.

LEADERSHIP AXIOM #204

Leaders are ready when opportunity knocks.
They don't knock the opportunity.

LEADERSHIP AXIOM #205

*Leaders live by the three Rs: **R**esponsibility, **R**esolve, **R**esiliency.*

LEADERSHIP AXIOM #206

Leaders promote the three Ps:
***P**roductivity, **P**rofessionalism, **P**erformance.*

LEADERSHIP AXIOM #207

Leaders know that if they want to be a good speaker,
they begin by being a good listener.

LEADERSHIP AXIOM #208

Leaders apply the three "tions": Motivation, Dedication, Completion.

LEADERSHIP AXIOM #209

Leaders are "able": Capable, Dependable, Reliable.

LEADERSHIP AXIOM #210

Leaders have a case of the "ives":
Inquisitive, Aggressive, Responsive, Decisive.

LEADERSHIP AXIOM #211

Leaders are not always experts, but they are nearly always extroverts.

LEADERSHIP AXIOM #212

Leaders know that purpose gives meaning to efforts and results.

LEADERSHIP AXIOM #213

Leaders measure others by results, not by their intentions.

LEADERSHIP AXIOM #214

Leaders allow their followers to reach their full potential.

LEADERSHIP AXIOM #215

Leaders are planners, not schemers.

LEADERSHIP AXIOM #216

Leaders know there are times when you need to stop chopping wood so you can sharpen the ax.

LEADERSHIP AXIOM #217

Leaders know more gets done when they issue compliments rather than complaints.

LEADERSHIP AXIOM #218

Leaders know you don't spell team with an "I."

LEADERSHIP AXIOM #219

Leaders work to find solutions, not fault.

LEADERSHIP AXIOM #220

Leaders respect others—they don't ridicule others.

LEADERSHIP AXIOM #221

Leaders are intellectually curious, not intellectually stagnant.

LEADERSHIP AXIOM #222

Leaders assist others—they don't resist others.

LEADERSHIP AXIOM #223

Leaders know that decisiveness is not inflexibility.

LEADERSHIP AXIOM #224

Leaders have a sense of humor:
Hope, **U**nity, **M**emory, **O**penness, **R**eason.

LEADERSHIP AXIOM #225

Leaders don't just see the big picture—they paint the picture.

LEADERSHIP AXIOM #226

*Leaders know that when they become comfortable
they become vulnerable.*

LEADERSHIP AXIOM #227

*Leaders know that consensus is not always achievable,
but it does not hinder their resolve.*

LEADERSHIP AXIOM #228

Leaders appreciate their people—they don't depreciate their people.

LEADERSHIP AXIOM #229

Leaders support their people—they don't sabotage them.

LEADERSHIP AXIOM #230

Leaders are problem solvers, not problem makers.

LEADERSHIP AXIOM #231

Leaders are encouraging, not discouraging.

LEADERSHIP AXIOM #232

Leaders rely on rectitude and shun decrepitude.

LEADERSHIP AXIOM #233

Leaders are purveyors of hope.

LEADERSHIP AXIOM #234

Leaders live—they don't just exist.

LEADERSHIP AXIOM #235

Leaders can think both strategically and tactically.

LEADERSHIP AXIOM #236

Leaders lead for the future, not just for the present.

LEADERSHIP AXIOM #237

Leaders manage stress—they are not managed by it.

LEADERSHIP AXIOM #238

Leaders are mental jugglers.

LEADERSHIP AXIOM #239

Leaders don't get bogged down in administrivia.

LEADERSHIP AXIOM #240

Leaders confront problems, not people.

LEADERSHIP AXIOM #241

Leaders know the best judgment is self-judgment.

LEADERSHIP AXIOM #242

Leaders possess wit: **W**hatever **I**t **T**akes.

LEADERSHIP AXIOM #243

Leaders open their minds before they open their mouths.

LEADERSHIP AXIOM #244

Leaders know that "winning" starts with "beginning."

LEADERSHIP AXIOM #245

There is one quality leaders can't do without—self-esteem.

LEADERSHIP AXIOM #246

Leaders don't let a bad experience make them bitter.
They know it makes them better.

LEADERSHIP AXIOM #247

Leaders don't tolerate mediocrity.
They know mediocrity is a step toward degeneration.

LEADERSHIP AXIOM #248

Leaders know that an improvement in attitude is a daily endeavor.

LEADERSHIP AXIOM #249

Leaders know success comes in "cans."
It doesn't come in "can'ts" or "cannots."

LEADERSHIP AXIOM #250

Leaders put their hearts in their organizations
and their organizations in their hearts.

LEADERSHIP AXIOM #251

Leaders keep their minds on their responsibilities
and their responsibilities on their minds.

LEADERSHIP AXIOM #252

Leaders know that training is learning "to do."
Education is learning "to think."

LEADERSHIP AXIOM #253

Leaders don't answer impossible questions.

LEADERSHIP AXIOM #254

Leaders know that consistency can often be as valuable as accuracy.

LEADERSHIP AXIOM #255

Leaders know that a "policy" is not a regulation.

LEADERSHIP AXIOM #256

*Leaders do not have an "open door" policy.
They have an "accessible door" policy.*

LEADERSHIP AXIOM #257

*Leaders know that work is what one "gets" to do,
not what one "has" to do.*

LEADERSHIP AXIOM #258

Leaders know that nothing succeeds like success.

LEADERSHIP AXIOM #259

Leaders manage conflict. They don't let conflict manage them.

LEADERSHIP AXIOM #260

*Leaders know a poor plan well executed is superior
to a good plan poorly executed.*

LEADERSHIP AXIOM #261

*Leaders think in both abstract and concrete terms,
but they don't allow themselves to get stuck in concrete.*

LEADERSHIP AXIOM #262

*Leaders know the best competition is to compete
against your own best achievements.*

LEADERSHIP AXIOM #263

*Leaders know leadership is not unidirectional.
It flows up as well as down.*

LEADERSHIP AXIOM #264

*Leaders know it's never too late to improve.
They also know it's never too early.*

LEADERSHIP AXIOM #265

Leaders don't sacrifice leadership for companionship.

LEADERSHIP AXIOM #266

Leaders don't sacrifice effect for affect.

LEADERSHIP AXIOM #267

Leaders don't sacrifice report for rapport.

LEADERSHIP AXIOM #268

Leaders don't sacrifice conclusion for occlusion.

LEADERSHIP AXIOM #269

Leaders believe right is might.

LEADERSHIP AXIOM #270

Leaders know that substance is far more important than appearance.

LEADERSHIP AXIOM #271

Leaders prefer work horses to show horses.

LEADERSHIP AXIOM #272

Leaders know that professionalism and rectitude are contagious.

LEADERSHIP AXIOM #273

Leaders know some things are best accomplished in a group setting. Other things are best accomplished in an individual setting.

LEADERSHIP AXIOM #274

Leaders know that a group personality is different from the sum of the individual group members' personalities.

LEADERSHIP AXIOM #275

Leaders know they don't establish a control system that costs more than the asset it's designed to protect.

LEADERSHIP AXIOM #276

Leaders know that first impressions are lasting impressions.

LEADERSHIP AXIOM #277

Leaders know that in a group setting the notion of impossibility is reduced.

LEADERSHIP AXIOM #278

Leaders know that in a group setting the group is inclined toward bravado and exaggeration.

LEADERSHIP AXIOM #279

Leaders know that a group setting is conducive to polarized thinking.

LEADERSHIP AXIOM #280

Leaders know that a group will structure itself with respect to the roles participants will play in meetings.

LEADERSHIP AXIOM #281

Leaders know that groups rely heavily on icons and symbols.

LEADERSHIP AXIOM #282

Leaders know that a changing situation can influence both leader and group behavior.

LEADERSHIP AXIOM #283

Leaders know there is a difference between possessing character and being a character.

LEADERSHIP AXIOM #284

Leaders know the wisest investment they can ever make is in human capital.

LEADERSHIP AXIOM #285

Leaders who have good people sense usually have good financial cents.

LEADERSHIP AXIOM #286

*Leaders know they need to read people with as much facility
as they read literature.*

LEADERSHIP AXIOM #287

*Leaders know that productivity is not a numbers concept.
It is a value concept.*

LEADERSHIP AXIOM #288

Leaders want profits:
People **R**eturning **O**ften **F**or **I**nsured **T**otal **S**atisfaction.

LEADERSHIP AXIOM #289

*Leaders know they can never defend a wrong,
but often what's right needs a lot of offense.*

LEADERSHIP AXIOM #290

Leaders make defining moments fine moments.

LEADERSHIP AXIOM #291

Leaders know the best motivation of all is self-motivation.

LEADERSHIP AXIOM #292

*Leaders know that motivation is both a prelude to,
and a sustainer of, action.*

LEADERSHIP AXIOM #293

Leaders don't raise their voices—they raise expectations.

LEADERSHIP AXIOM #294

Leaders know that life is full of surprises, but they never act surprised.

LEADERSHIP AXIOM #295

Leaders know there is a difference between being an exception and being exceptional.

LEADERSHIP AXIOM #296

Leaders listen to what people are saying, but they also listen for what people are not saying.

LEADERSHIP AXIOM #297

Leaders don't sacrifice statesmanship for gamesmanship.

LEADERSHIP AXIOM #298

Leaders know that not all leadership styles work in every situation.

LEADERSHIP AXIOM #299

Leaders don't set constraints—they set challenges.

LEADERSHIP AXIOM #300

Leaders know there is a difference between solutions and resolutions.

LEADERSHIP AXIOM #301

Leaders recruit for a breadth of talent, not a depth of staff.

LEADERSHIP AXIOM #302

*Leaders know there is a difference between serving people
and processing people.*

LEADERSHIP AXIOM #303

Leaders know they must prepare their followers for the future.

LEADERSHIP AXIOM #304

True leaders have a "seventh sense" as to when they need to "turn over the reins."

LEADERSHIP AXIOM #305

Leaders know they must develop "benchstrength"— people who can take over at a moment's notice.

LEADERSHIP AXIOM #306

Leaders cause their organizations to soar, not sour.

LEADERSHIP AXIOM #307

Leaders know it is the customer who pays their salaries.

LEADERSHIP AXIOM #308

Leaders know it's not "who you are" but "what you do."

LEADERSHIP AXIOM #309

Leaders know their organizations must strive for continual renewal.

LEADERSHIP AXIOM #310

Leaders are expert translators. They translate vision into reality.

LEADERSHIP AXIOM #311

Leaders know the most tragic deception of all is self-deception.

LEADERSHIP AXIOM #312

Leadership is evident when achievement occurs without the leader being present.

LEADERSHIP AXIOM #313

Leaders surround themselves with people of equal or greater ability.

LEADERSHIP AXIOM #314

Leaders know there is no shame in getting knocked down.
The shame is in not getting back up.

LEADERSHIP AXIOM #315

Leaders don't eschew diversity. They embrace it.

LEADERSHIP AXIOM #316

Leaders don't chafe at competition. They conquer it.

LEADERSHIP AXIOM #317

*Leaders espouse the three Vs: **V**eracity, **V**alor, **V**ersatility.*

LEADERSHIP AXIOM #318

Leaders strive for the maximum possible, not the minimum allowable.

LEADERSHIP AXIOM #319

Leaders don't lead for the sake of leading.
They lead for the sake of serving.

LEADERSHIP AXIOM #320

Leaders energize their people—they don't enervate them.

LEADERSHIP AXIOM #321

Leaders overcome resistance to change by assisting in change.

LEADERSHIP AXIOM #322

Leaders build realizable expectations.

LEADERSHIP AXIOM #323

Leaders know it is better to underpromise and overdeliver.

LEADERSHIP AXIOM #324

Leaders make their own luck: **L**everage, **U**tility, **C**ourage, **K**arma.

LEADERSHIP AXIOM #325

*Leaders experience the selflessness and satisfaction
of human achievement. They also experience the tragedy
and treachery of human weakness.*

LEADERSHIP AXIOM #326

Leaders believe in zero defects. They also believe in zero defaults.

LEADERSHIP AXIOM #327

Leaders light "a fire" in the belly of the constituency.

LEADERSHIP AXIOM #328

Leaders seek to make a difference.

LEADERSHIP AXIOM #329

Good leaders don't need to issue numerous directives.

LEADERSHIP AXIOM #330

Leaders know the best incentive they can give to their people is growth.

LEADERSHIP AXIOM #331

Leaders are trustees of the future.

LEADERSHIP AXIOM #332

*Leaders see connections between and among things
that others only see as unrelated events.*

LEADERSHIP AXIOM #333

*Leaders know participative management is not democratic
management. It's receiving input but reserving the right
of decision making.*

LEADERSHIP AXIOM #334

Leaders know people don't respond nearly as well to threats
as they respond to challenges.

LEADERSHIP AXIOM #335

Leaders don't sacrifice product for process.

LEADERSHIP AXIOM #336

Leaders are book smart. They are also street smart.

LEADERSHIP AXIOM #337

Leaders know their own strengths and weaknesses.
They fortify the former and complement the latter.

LEADERSHIP AXIOM #338

Leaders convert dissatisfaction into satisfaction.

LEADERSHIP AXIOM #339

Leaders know there are times when they have to go out on a limb,
but they don't give others a saw.

LEADERSHIP AXIOM #340

Leaders are multi-tasked, but they are also multi-talented.

LEADERSHIP AXIOM #341

Successful leadership does not just reside at headquarters.
It flows down to the footquarters.

LEADERSHIP AXIOM #342

Leaders have a high I.Q.: Inherent Quality.

LEADERSHIP AXIOM #343

Leaders align group behavior with group objectives.

LEADERSHIP AXIOM #344

Leaders anticipate, participate, radiate, and consummate.

LEADERSHIP AXIOM #345

*Leaders, of necessity, must accept imperfection,
but they still don't tolerate imperfection.*

LEADERSHIP AXIOM #346

Leaders believe in service: Spirit, Enthusiasm, Responsibility, Values, Inspiration, Cooperation, Excellence.

LEADERSHIP AXIOM #347

Leaders know that uncertainty breeds anxiety. Certainty breeds resolution.

LEADERSHIP AXIOM #348

Leaders know that there is value in symbolism.

LEADERSHIP AXIOM #349

Leaders know biology is not destiny. Personality is destiny.

LEADERSHIP AXIOM #350

Leaders structure frameworks for people to "buy" ideas rather than be "sold" ideas.

LEADERSHIP AXIOM #351

Leaders know persistence is preferred to insistence.

LEADERSHIP AXIOM #352

*Leaders know that once they have lost their integrity,
there is nothing left.*

LEADERSHIP AXIOM #353

Leaders rely on the five As: **A***bility,* **A***cceptance,* **A***ction,*
A*ssistance,* **A***ccountability.*

LEADERSHIP AXIOM #354

*Leaders know that fear of failure can be surmounted
by building a foundation for the future.*

LEADERSHIP AXIOM #355

*Leaders know they are most effective when they are **not** in the limelight.*

LEADERSHIP AXIOM #356

True leaders possess ethics:
Ethical **T**enets **H**ave **I**nherently **C**ommanding **S**trength.

LEADERSHIP AXIOM #357

Leaders possess drive:
Determination, **R**easoning, **I**nnovation, **V**alidation, **E**quanimity.

Leadership Axiom #358

Leaders know that they can only be as effective as their followers allow them to be.

Leadership Axiom #359

*Leaders are aware of the seven Ds: **D**ecisions **D**emand **D**evotion to **D**uty, **D**edication, and **D**eciphering of **D**etail.*

Leadership Axiom #360

Leaders don't "obstaclize" their people. They "facilitize" them.

LEADERSHIP AXIOM #361

Leaders avoid the seven deadly sins of leadership: Arrogance, Insensitivity, Myopia, Sloth, Misrepresentation, Greed, Addictions.

LEADERSHIP AXIOM #362

Leaders know there are times when they must be strong in their restraint.

LEADERSHIP AXIOM #363

Leaders value time: **T***act,* **I***nformation,* **M***otivation,* **E***ffectiveness.*

LEADERSHIP AXIOM #364

True leaders don't seek personal memorials.
They seek organizational memorials.

LEADERSHIP AXIOM #365

Leaders know the most noble word in any language is "teach."
The most challenging word in any language is "learn."

LEADERSHIP AXIOM #366

Leaders know perfection is a value, not an object.

LEADERSHIP AXIOM #367

Leaders know there is no "bottom line" without a "top line."

LEADERSHIP AXIOM #368

Leaders know that it is their attitude that is the cornerstone of their success.

LEADERSHIP AXIOM #369

A test of a leader's efficiency is how well the group remains united and focused on the objective.

LEADERSHIP AXIOM #370

Leaders must, at times, turn their backs to their followers.

LEADERSHIP AXIOM #371

A fundamental principle of civilization is that people require leadership.

LEADERSHIP AXIOM #372

Leaders exude an indomitable spirit.

LEADERSHIP AXIOM #373

Leaders look for VIPs: **V***itality,* **I***ntuition,* **P***rogress,* **S***uccess.*

LEADERSHIP AXIOM #374

Strong leaders have long and strong memories.

LEADERSHIP AXIOM #375

Leaders don't jump to conclusions—they jump to opportunities.

LEADERSHIP AXIOM #376

Leaders don't throw tirades—they throw tenets.

LEADERSHIP AXIOM #377

Leaders don't pound their fists. They pound out solutions.

LEADERSHIP AXIOM #378

Leaders don't beat a dead horse. They beat the odds.

LEADERSHIP AXIOM #379

Leaders don't excise exercise.

LEADERSHIP AXIOM #380

Leaders don't manipulate people. They accelerate them.

LEADERSHIP AXIOM #381

Leaders obliterate obstacles.

LEADERSHIP AXIOM #382

Leaders don't press their luck. They press for results.

LEADERSHIP AXIOM #383

*Leaders know if they look after pennies,
the dollars will look after themselves.*

LEADERSHIP AXIOM #384

Leaders know that half truths are also half false.

LEADERSHIP AXIOM #385

Leaders are careful about running contests—
they know there can be more losers than winners.

LEADERSHIP AXIOM #386

Leaders are gracious in receiving compliments,
but they are also a little suspicious.

LEADERSHIP AXIOM #387

A leader's primordial wish: Follow Me.

LEADERSHIP AXIOM #388

*Leaders enjoy banking: banking on themselves
and banking on their people.*

LEADERSHIP AXIOM #389

Leaders are not dumb: Deceptive, Unaware: Malevolent, Bellicose.

LEADERSHIP AXIOM #390

Leaders know that their ethics are the exclamation points of their life.

LEADERSHIP AXIOM #391

Leaders know that strategy is an eight-step process. Survey, Tactics, Resources, Assumptions, Testing, Execution, Growth, Yield.

LEADERSHIP AXIOM #392

Leaders are proactive, active, and reactive.

LEADERSHIP AXIOM #393

Leaders believe in living: Loyalty, Integrity, Vision, Inspiration, Navigation, Growth.

LEADERSHIP AXIOM #394

Leaders don't stomp their feet. They stomp out problems.

LEADERSHIP AXIOM #395

Leaders know there are times when the best action to take is no action.

LEADERSHIP AXIOM #396

Leaders don't yell. They tell.

LEADERSHIP AXIOM #397

Leaders know there is a direct, positive correlation between high morale and the follower's belief in them.

LEADERSHIP AXIOM #398

Leaders know teamwork consists of two letters: **WE.**

LEADERSHIP AXIOM #399

Leaders think like a clear speaker and speak like a clear thinker.

LEADERSHIP AXIOM #400

Leaders know that being at the top requires them to get to the bottom.

LEADERSHIP AXIOM #401

Leaders know "good enough"—isn't.

LEADERSHIP AXIOM #402

Leaders know there are times when the most important message they can deliver is to say nothing.

LEADERSHIP AXIOM #403

Leaders don't use hammers. They use tillers.

LEADERSHIP AXIOM #404

Leaders should ask themselves, "Would I follow me?"

LEADERSHIP AXIOM #405

Leaders need followers like fire needs oxygen.

LEADERSHIP AXIOM #406

There are two kinds of people—those who lead and those who let them.

LEADERSHIP AXIOM #407

Leaders are born everyday—some just never come alive.

LEADERSHIP AXIOM #408

Leadership means being the first in the fray and the last to be fed.

LEADERSHIP AXIOM #409

Avoid the leader who looks for power.
Rush to the leader who looks to serve.

LEADERSHIP AXIOM #410

A mob is a leaderless crowd.
A movement begins when a leader steps up.

LEADERSHIP AXIOM #411

The first test of leadership is to see if anyone is following.

LEADERSHIP AXIOM #412

*Leadership was born when the first human pointed and said,
"I think we should go over there," and everyone did.*

LEADERSHIP AXIOM #413

*Leaders know there is a difference between intelligence and wisdom.
The former is "raw material," and the latter is "finished product."*

LEADERSHIP AXIOM #414

Great ideas demand great leadership.

LEADERSHIP AXIOM #415

Leaders know history can be a harbinger.

LEADERSHIP AXIOM #416

Old leaders never die—their spirits remain.

LEADERSHIP AXIOM #417

The world is not lacking in leadership.
The world is lacking in an understanding of leadership.

THE TRANSITION

"Well, Redael, there you have them, all 417 of my Leadership Axioms," said Winning Wizard, eyes twinkling. "I hope they will benefit you as much as they did me," the sage said with a trace of hope.

"Utterly fantastic, Winning Wizard, absolutely fantastic," Redael proclaimed. "I feel as though I have just had a leadership blood transfusion. I can see things in an entirely new light now," said the young executive, feeling reborn and exhilarated. "Those are powerful axioms. I will read one every day, and yes, I will read two on Mondays."

"I'm glad you feel that way, Redael," Winning Wizard quipped. "If you develop the mindset of a leader, there is no end to the possibilities that await you. As a matter of fact, I better tell you Winning Wizard's Words of Management Wisdom #117 to bring the points home to you:

THE WIZARD'S WORDS OF MANAGEMENT WISDOM #117

Using the leadership axioms allows you to transition from a manager with administrative responsibilities to a leader with management responsibilities."

"I will remember and use these axioms, Winning Wizard, I promise you that, because I truly want to become an outstanding leader," replied an exuberant Redael. "Thank you ever so much, Winning Wizard, ever so much."

Epilogue

R EDAEL RECEIVED THE NEWS OF THE MAJOR PROMOTION
the next week. Winning Wizard called to offer resounding congrat-
ulations and to offer any assistance Redael requested.

Two years passed quickly. Redael read a Leadership Axiom, or two,
every day and felt invigorated by the words and meanings contained
therein. Redael also continued to meet the challenges that arose, some
of which were handled artfully and others of which were handled, well,
shall we say, not so artfully. Redael wondered if another conversation
with Winning Wizard would prove beneficial. "I may give Winning Wizard a call just to say hello," Redael thought, "I may just do that."

Winning Wizard kept abreast of Redael's career performance and progression and was silently pleased with the results, feeling a sense of
contribution and of having left an intellectual legacy. "It's been a cou-
ple of years since Redael and I got together for a conversation," Winning Wizard reminisced. "Perhaps I should call Redael just to check up
on things. I really should."

Index